Maximizing Manhood

Beating the Male Menopause

Malcolm Carruthers, MD, FRC Path, MRCGP

■ HarperCollins*Publishers*

To the father – in his many forms

HarperCollins*Publishers*
77–85 Fulham Palace Road,
Hammersmith, London W6 8JB

Originally published in hardback by
HarperCollins as *Male Menopause* in1996
Paperback edition 1997

10 9 8 7 6 5 4 3 2

© Malcolm Carruthers 1996

Malcolm Carruthers asserts the moral right
to be identified as the author of this work

A catalogue record for this book
is available from the British Library

ISBN 0 7225 3532 5

Printed in Great Britain by
Caledonian International Book Manufacturing Ltd,
Glasgow

Contents

Foreword

Dr Malcolm Carruthers' first book, *The Western Way of Death: Stress, Tension and Heart Disease*, on stress in modern life and its effect on the factors which can lead to heart disease, has influenced medical and lay thinking ever since.

His new book, *Maximizing Manhood: Beating the Male Menopause*, on the declining vitality of men once they pass middle age, and the part which lack of testosterone has in this, is of equal importance, and will also be read as avidly by doctors as their patients. Hormone replacement for men needs as careful consideration as HRT for women.

Malcolm Carruthers' case that the lack of drive, enthusiasm and libido which is now accepted as being the lot of men in their late 50s and 60s, in fact in many cases is a result of insufficient testosterone activity, is well made. The evidence that testosterone treatment, when carefully supervised, is safe seems sound, but still has to be finally proved.

Dr Carruthers writes with authority which is not diminished by his very readable style. This scholarly book is well-researched and includes fascinating internationally-gathered medical detail which will intrigue and inform professional and lay readers in all parts of the world.

Dr Thomas Stuttaford OBE
Medical Columnist
The Times

Acknowledgements

Help is gratefully acknowledged in three areas: in the production of this book, Jane Graham-Maw, Editor-at-Large, took it through the earlier stages of publication and her successor, Wanda Whiteley, eased it skillfully through the later ones. Elizabeth Hutchins rapidly and efficiently edited the manuscript, and made this stage of open book surgery relatively painless. The whole HarperCollins publishing team have been a pleasure to work with throughout.

In the professional level, I was encouraged to write this book by Gail Sheehy on her visit to England in 1992 while researching her own book, *New Passages*, also published by HarperCollins this year. It is hoped that this will give medical backing to her work in helping men as well as women to cope with the historic changes in their life-cycles, particularly the Second Adulthood in middle life.

The medical research on which this work is based was supported partly by grants from the European Organization for the Control of Circulatory Diseases (EOCCD) and the Sophus Jacobsen og hustru Astrid Jacobsen's

Fond and LBK Foundation in Copenhagen, Denmark, as well as Drs Jens Moller and Michael Hansen, previous and current presidents of these organizations.

The author also wishes to thank Dr Jamie Zadeh, Doreen Jackson and Graham Carter of the Department of Endocrinology at the Charing Cross Hospital, London, where the pathology tests were performed; Professor Vivian James of the Department of Steroid Endocrinology, St Mary's Hospital, London; Mr Neil O'Donoghue of the Institute of Urology, London, and Col Douglas W Soderdahl FACS, Chief of Urology, the Honolulu Medical Group, for constructive advice and criticism.

On the personal level, my brother Dr Barry Carruthers influenced my choice of career and sparked my interest in andrology. Dr Janet Carruthers gave me the opportunity to experience the joys of fatherhood, as did my three sons Ian, Andrew and Robert, who gave helpful comments on earlier versions of this book. Vera and Louise Diamond, and Gurumayi Chidvilasananda, showed me the power of the mother to shape men's lives. Jean Coleman gave me the peace of mind to write, and Cynthia Read also provided kind assistance in editing the text.

Finally, my thanks are due to many of my patients whose experiences are recorded here, particularly those who were brave and supportive enough to 'stand up and be counted' in the newspapers, radio and television. Special thanks are due to Bernard Collen and his wife Michele, to James Savin, Robert Bain and Spencer Churchill. When the 'Male Menopause' is finally accepted as a biological fact of life for some men, and male HRT becomes a standard method of treatment and an accepted part of preventive medicine, they will have made a great contribution.

The Male Menopause Mystery

What is the mystery of the male menopause? It is the mystery of why the vitality and virility of millions of men go missing in middle age or later. It is the mystery of why most people and their doctors deny, ignore or unquestioningly accept this disappearance – and of why no attempt is made to investigate the losses or even reclaim them, despite evidence that this is often possible.

As in most detective stories, the answer lies in asking the right questions and hopefully finding the right answers, piecing together the jigsaw until the picture leaps out at you. Many investigators have already searched the area for many years without stumbling over the truth. Let's start with a few questions and think about the clues we might follow up to find the answers.

What's Gone Missing?

The typical story is of a man in middle age who gradually loses his drive, strength, energy and enthusiasm for life and love. Action man has become inaction man. An all-enveloping mental and physical tiredness descends on him, often for no apparent reason. He changes from being a positive, bullish, outgoing person who it is good to be around to a negative, pessimistic, depressed bear with a sore head and it is increasingly difficult to live or work with him. At work he is seen to have 'gone off the boil' and no amount of encouragement or urging will improve his performance. At home, family relations tend to become increasingly strained, and social life and activities dwindle and wilt. His sexual life is usually a disaster area, with loss of libido and intermittent failure to achieve an erection leading to performance anxiety and eventually complete impotence. This creates a downward spiral of failing function in both boardroom and bedroom.

When, after ignoring or denying his condition for months or even years, the quietly desperate man goes to see a doctor, all he is told is, 'So you feel tired, dispirited, exhausted and your sex life is non-existent? It's your age. I feel like that, too. What do you expect? So your wife had the same symptoms when she went through the menopause and got hormones from her gynaecologist which revitalized her so much that you can't keep up? That doesn't apply to *you* – there's no such thing as the male menopause or male hormone replacement therapy. Just forget it and take these anti-depressants – they'll make us both feel better.'

Why the Denial?

Why do neither doctors nor patients recognize the male menopause as a real medical condition worthy of being diagnosed and treated? Because, even if dignified with the medical title of 'andropause', as it is known in Europe, it is still an unacceptable threat to their macho self-image. It is the joke disorder attributed to any middle-aged male character in a sit-com who behaves in an unexpected or irrational fashion. Men see it as the end of their lives as potent males, as leaders and as lovers.

While the female menopause usually happens in the limited age range of about 45–55, the symptoms in men can start any time from 30 onwards, though they too tend to peak at 50. Interestingly, 50, the 'Big Five-O', appears to be a watershed in the lives of both men and women. Yet this should be simply half-time in the game of life, the goal being 100 years of activity and enjoyment! Why do men put up with losing so much so young?

Gail Sheehy, an American authoress who has written a fascinating book on life cycles in both men and women, *New Passages*,[1] describes the male menopause as the 'unspeakable passage'[2]. While women are willing to discuss their menopause with each other and with their medical advisers, men are remarkably reluctant to turn to either unless desperate. In fact they are likely to get very angry with anyone, even their nearest and dearest, who might suggest that they need any treatment. If cancer is the unmentionable 'Big C', the male menopause is the even more inadmissible 'Big M'.

Logically, there should be no shame attached to this condition. Indeed, as we shall see later, it is often the many 'hammer blows of fate' involved in living life to the full which cause it. The most macho of males can suffer from it. But even men who have greatly improved with testosterone treatment will rarely go public for fear of being thought weak or ridiculed by their friends or relatives. Fortunately there are an increasing number who are willing to stand up and be counted, and they greatly help recognition of the condition and its treatment by doing so.

Why Has Testosterone Had Such a Bad Press?

Another problem is the public perception of testosterone. It is widely held to be the hormone responsible for undesirable male traits such as aggression and hypersexuality. So surely testosterone replacement therapy (TRT) will 'bring out the beast'? The fear, in practice unfounded, of becoming a rapacious monster like Jack Nicholson in the film 'Wolf' holds back from treatment many menopausal men who, unlike him, cannot claim to have 'retained my testosterone longer than most males'.

Also, reports of the abuse of anabolic steroids by athletes and body-builders, together with deliberately exaggerated horror stories of their physical and psychological dangers, have appeared in the newspapers at increasingly frequent intervals over the last 20 years.[3,4] As testosterone is the basic compound from which all the other anabolic steroids are derived, it has suffered a very bad press by association.

Why Isn't Biotechnology Coming Up with the Answers?

Linked with these factors is the extreme reluctance of most drug firms to consider funding research into testosterone replacement therapy for men, even though oestrogen replacement therapy for women is a rapidly expanding market, already estimated to be worth over £50 million annually.

The existing testosterone preparations, many of which have proved safe and successful for up to 50 years, are now out of their product licences, so that anyone can make them and profit margins are smaller. There is also the risk of litigation by patients suffering side-effects, particularly in the USA. These sex hormones just aren't sexy any more. Even so, foresight would suggest the potential market is vast and more convenient long-acting forms are urgently needed to make TRT more popular, more economic and more easily available. Yet most doctors interested in developing new forms of testosterone treatment have experienced the extreme apathy or even antipathy of pharmaceutical companies.

Why Shouldn't We Just Grow Old 'Gracefully'?

Many doctors, politicians and economists argue that no country could afford the cost of this 'his and hers HRT' and who wants to keep an increasing number of 'golden oldies' going anyway? It isn't natural.

Yet women over the last 30 years or more have fought successfully to maintain their hormonal status into later life, with all the consequent medical benefits. Supporters of 'men's lib' would say that they have up to now been sadly neglected, they have a seven or eight-year shorter life expectancy than women as it is and it's time they had a chance of catching up in the health stakes.

There are also many good reasons for regarding 'his and hers HRT' as an important part of the preventive medicine of the future, helping both sexes to prolong an active and enjoyable life. It adds life to years as well as years to life. Health economic theorists have also pointed out that substantial savings can be made by shortening the terminal period of disability and incapacity, which would give many people a happier ending to life.

Of course something is going to fail at some time in one of our body's systems, but shouldn't we at least be looking at every reasonable option for staying as mentally and physically active as we can, for as long as possible? The benefits have to be weighed against costs and dangers, but doctors should be continually assessing the evidence for and against each treatment and offering it to the patients to decide for themselves, not prejudging the issues.

Given the wide range of benefits to psyche, soma and sexuality, increasing numbers of people see hormone therapy more as modern science giving nature a helping hand.

Why Doesn't Medical Science Recognize the Problem?

The reasons for this are many and varied. They illustrate very well how ideas come into fashion and go out of style in a cyclical way.

Medical theory does not seem to advance in a straight line, but in a series of loops. It's as though while wandering in the sands of time scientists come across facts from which they make up a theory which is then taught to students and other doctors until they cease to question it. The theory is then 'in'. Taking that as their starting-point, the scientists trudge on round the loop, gathering more facts, until they find some which seem to contradict the original theory. That is then regarded as simplistic, false and definitely 'out'. Never mind, change the teaching, change the textbooks and go on, regardless.

Then the scientists rediscover some of the footprints in the sand left by those who originally thought up the theory which lead right back to the starting-point. To avoid the worrying realization that they've just walked in a complete circle, they add a few new facts to prove it right after all. The old theory is dusted down, prettied up with a glamorous statistical wig to cover a few bald facts and some reference make-up, and comes right back 'in' again.

In case you think I exaggerate a little, let me give you

a brief account of the curious history of theories about whether the male menopause is a real or imaginary condition.

Ideas about what gives a man both vitality and virility, and why these qualities vary from person to person and at different stages in life, are as old as recorded history. Certainly, at the end of the eighteenth century the concept of the male menopause or 'decline' as it was then called, was definitely 'in'. A Dr Hooper, living in London, wrote in his *Medical Dictionary*, 'Decline in men is a real malady and not a natural or constitutional decay, as is perfectly obvious from recovery.'[5] He had observed that men could sometimes make a remarkable recovery when their businesses prospered or a new woman came into their lives.

About 100 years later attempts were made to rejuvenate older men by injecting testicular extracts and even whole testes from different species. In general these 'monkey gland' treatments, as they became known, got a bad name because they were usually ineffective and were largely practised by quacks out to make a fast buck out of old bucks. These practices discredited the idea of the male menopause and its treatment, which then went 'out', and left stains upon the good name of testosterone which persist to this day.

It was only when testosterone was isolated and then synthesized in industrial quantities from 1935 onwards that effective replacement therapy with this hormone became possible. This brought theories about the male menopause or 'male climacteric' – another medical term for decline – back into favour again and for a time everything was straightforward and scientifically respectable.

Excellent articles and books appeared in the medical literature of the 1940s, accurately documenting the symptoms of the male menopause and noting how similar they were to those of the female menopause. This is why the name has stuck, even though it is inappropriate and has held up acceptance and treatment of the condition it describes. Not only were the symptoms clear cut, but the cause was shown to be insufficient testosterone for the body's needs, because the amount of testosterone which overflowed into the urine went down with age and other hormones from the pituitary gland went up to try to stimulate its production.

Some of the most conclusive evidence comes from this period. A remarkably modern 'blind' trial was reported in the prestigious *Journal of the American Medical Association* in 1944.[6] There, testosterone injections were clearly shown to rapidly and dramatically relieve the symptoms of the male menopause, while placebo injections of the carrier sesame oil did not.

An editorial in the same issue gave the official blessing:

> *The facts that are here cited serve to indicate with increasing probability that the male climacteric is just as truly a syndrome based on endocrine disturbances as is the menopause syndrome in women.*[7]

The same year, as well as this medical recognition came an explanatory article in the *Reader's Digest Magazine* making it clear to the *lay* public that the condition and its treatment were established facts. This was followed in 1945 by a powerful book by an American writer, Paul de Kruif, called *The Male Hormone: A new gleam of hope for prolonging man's prime of life*.[8] This detailed how theories relating to testosterone treatments rose and fell and rose again, and made a compelling case for its widespread use. Game, set and match to the male menopause activists! What could possibly go wrong?

Well, fashions change. After a few years, more sensitive chemical tests were introduced which could measure the minute amounts of various hormones in the blood, including testosterone. It was then found that the total amount of testosterone in the blood of most men did not decrease much with age. It was therefore argued that while women at the menopause showed a dramatic fall in blood oestrogen levels which would account for their symptoms, men did not and therefore their symptoms must be imaginary.

Male menopause detractors also bracketed its symptoms with the emotional upheavals of the 'male mid-life crisis'. The latter is an existential, emotional crisis, not a hormonal one, and the two need to be clearly distinguished. More on this later.

For the last 25 years, because of conflicting evidence surrounding the male menopause theory, the majority of doctors have ignored or derided it.[9] With more up-to-date and detailed research information, and a re-assessment of the mass of supportive facts which can be gathered from the literature and recent clinical experience, however, I hope to re-establish the concept and the benefits of treatment once and for all. I am convinced it is an idea whose time has come.

Chapter One

The Testosterone Story

Hormones have a long, exciting and chequered history, and testosterone has the longest, most exciting and most chequered of all. This is part of the problem in getting the male menopause accepted as a real condition, so let's look back to see where the maze of myths surrounding testosterone started.

Antiquity

Castration Makes the Eunuch

This observation, properly credited to primitive man, ushered in the dawn of hormone research.[1] To emulate one of Sir Winston Churchill's most famous sayings, 'Never in the field of human science was so much learned by so many by the removal of so little.'

As the American journalist Paul de Kruif put it in his historic book *The Male Hormone*, printed in 1945:

From the beginning of human record, priests, saints, medicine men, farmers and sultans had been demonstrat-

> *ing how clear-cut, sure and simple it was to take the vigour of animals and men away. How? By removing their testicles.*[2]

(Incidentally, de Kruif is another example of the wayward march of medical science. He asks, 'Why didn't they reason that older men, losing their youth gradually, might also be suffering a slow, chemical castration taking place invisibly with the passage of time?' Then he goes on to document how the 'hormone hunters' aim to rescue 'broken men' by isolating and then synthesizing testosterone. However, his message had to wait 50 years to be heard.)

Castration carried out on young boys was always recognized as preventing the onset of puberty, with lack of body hair or beard, more feminine fat distribution and a high-pitched voice much valued in singing. This was thought to be worth the sacrifice by some Italian singers, the *castrati*, or at least their managers, as graphically shown in the recent film *Farinelli, Il Castrato*. Eunuchs were also known not to develop the male pattern of baldness and to be less muscular.

Depending on how long after puberty it was performed, castration also reduced the eunuch's sexual and other drives, as well as making him infertile, but did not invariably make him lose erectile power. The more potent eunuchs used by Roman women, particularly when their husbands were away fighting for the Empire, for occupation without procreation.

Eunuchs were also known to be less competitive and aggressive. For the 1,000 years from about AD 400, the Byzantine Empire was run increasingly by eunuchs, who were efficient, but predictably unadventurous and did what they were told. They also played an important part in the administration of the Imperial Court. They presumably knew their place and posed no threat to the Emperor or those vying for power.

Similarly, farmers of antiquity knew that castration could be used to fatten pigs, bullocks and cockerels to produce capons. The taming of wild animals for domestic purposes and tempering the fiery nature of both horses and dogs made the psychological effects of castration in other species equally apparent.

The great physician Hippocrates, who is said to have created medicine as both an art and science, lived during the golden age of Greek culture, being born in 460 BC and dying at over 90 years of age. In the many classic writings noted by his pupils, he observed that gout does not appear before puberty, women do not develop it until after the 'menopause' and eunuchs not at all. Modern theory would suggest that the high levels of uric acid which cause this exquisitely painful condition of the joints come from the breakdown of the protein in the large muscle masses which testosterone produces in the postpubertal male.

Hippocrates also knew that mumps could be followed by the inflammation of the testes known as orchitis and then sterility. This can also contribute to an early onset of the male menopause *(see pages 96–7)*.

Judaic medicine meanwhile, derived from the Old Testament, held that health was the gift of God and disease his wrath. Ill-health could therefore only be prevented by submission, atonement, prayer, moral reform or sacrifice. It was also recognized, however, that stress, disease, fatigue and starvation could reduce the amount of semen. These are all factors now known to lower testosterone levels, particularly in older men.

The Bible differentiated between those who because of diseased or undescended testes developed eunuchoid features (known in Egypt as 'those castrated by Ra', the sun god, therefore 'sun-castrates') and those castrated by man ('man-castrates'). When castration was performed for religious reasons, the penis was often removed as well, a mutilation now only seen in some transsexuals.

The differentiation is described in Matthew 19:12, where Jesus is quoted as saying:

For there are some eunuchs, which were so born from their mother's womb: and there are some eunuchs, which were made eunuchs of men: and there be eunuchs which have made themselves eunuchs for the kingdom of heaven's sake.

In the latter category, he appears to be referring to priests who achieved celibacy without going to such extreme measures.

These causes of testicular insufficiency, or hypogonadism, are recognized today as either originating before birth or later in life following some damage to the testis or interference with the production or action of testosterone. The origins of the male menopause mainly fall within the secondary category, but occasionally there are elements of early factors which have been overlooked, as when one or both testes fail to develop or descend fully. Then there may be sufficient hormone to take the boy through an apparently normal puberty and even make him fertile, but in his thirties or forties the other factors which contribute to the menopause cause the limited supply of testosterone to become insufficient.

In India, from ancient times, those who renounce sexual activity because they believe it dissipates their spiritual energy have been known as *bramacharya*. In the Hindu tradition, this is one of the requirements of becoming a monk or Swami. A vegetarian diet may help them to make this difficult sacrifice and keep from straying from the spiritual path by decreasing the amount of cholesterol available for testosterone production.

This was confirmed in 1984 when a Swedish study showed that switching from a high to a low fat diet, particularly one high in polyunsaturates, lowered blood testosterone levels by 10 per cent.[3] This makes sense in evolutionary terms, as the aggressive killer instinct of the hunter, red in tooth and claw, would be enhanced by the higher level of testosterone produced by having a higher fat, higher cholesterol diet than the more placid herbivorous prey.

The beadle of the orphanage in Dickens's *Oliver Twist*, Mr Bumble, rebuked the undertaker who employed Oliver until he got into a fight with the words, '*You never should have given the boy meat. Meat heats the blood.*'

Perhaps the old man who for many years used to wander up and down Oxford Street in London with sandwich boards denouncing the 'passion proteins' in meat and declaring that they led to war may have stumbled upon an important truth.

Also, phytoestrogens, the oestrogens present in many plants, can antagonize the effects of testosterone and give a more female type of fat distribution. The plants richest in these phytoestrogens are soya, particularly tofu and miso, citrus fruits, wheat, liquorice, alfalfa, fennel and celery. This may be why some vegetarian yogis have enlarged breasts, a condition known as 'gynaecomastia', and large abdomens. Pliny recorded 2,000 years ago that '*Hempseed and chondrion make men impotent.*' Also, heavy beer drinkers, because of the phytoestrogens in hops, as well as the calories from the alcohol and its damaging effect on the testes and liver, can have enlarged breasts and a 'beer belly' as well as the erection problems described as 'brewer's droop'.

The most influential physician of Roman times was Galen (AD 130–200), who is considered the greatest medical man of antiquity after Hippocrates. He wrote more than 100 books, which dominated medical thinking for more than 1,500 years, well into the Renaissance period and beyond. However, he could also be thought of as the founding father of medical dogmatism in that his system was so authoritative and rigid that it almost completely stifled fresh ideas throughout that time.

In spite of this, Galen could be considered the forerunner of sex hormone theory and research. He describes how the 'maleness' of men could cease with castration and the 'femaleness' of women with disease or ageing of the ovaries. He noted that these sexual characteristics were generalized throughout the body in all the species he studied, and were not purely genital, being seen for example in the lion's mane, the cock's comb and the boar's tusk. These remote and widespread effects are the characteristic features of hormonal action.

Also, in his book *Peri Spermatos* ('On the Seed'), Galen raised a key question about the menopausal reduction of vitality: *'What is, therefore, the cause, that castrates slow down in their whole vital capacity?'* He remarks that castrated animals lose not only the power to procreate, but also the desire to do so, and that eunuchs showed the characteristic changes in normal male fat and hair distribution. In modern medical parlance, they show all the signs of testosterone deficiency.

The Medicinal Properties of Semen

Linked to observations on castration was the idea, fairly common throughout antiquity, that semen was beneficial to men's health.

About 4,000 years ago the *Pen Tsao*, the Chinese 'Great Herbal', recommended the use of the semen of young men for treating sexual weakness in the elderly, a remedy doubtless popular with the wives of the impotent potentates.

In India, the Hindu Ayervedic system of medicine which developed from 1400 BC onwards suggested the consumption of testicular tissue to treat impotence and obesity. It was also known at that time that hot baths could reduce fertility, which is still news over 3,000 years later.

Nearly 2,000 years ago, the Greek physician Pliny recommended eating animal testicles to improve sexual function. This remedy is still popular in many countries, especially Spain, where cooked bulls' testes are served as the delicacy known as *cojones*. Not coincidentally, this is also the Spanish word for courage. Unfortunately, any benefits obtained from eating such dishes are likely to be more morale boosting than hormone boosting, because though most of the body's supply of testosterone is made in the testes, it is rapidly exported to the rest of the body in the bloodstream and there is little on site at any one time.

For example, when chemists first extracted the hormone from bulls' testes in the early 1930s, it took several tons to produce a few hundred milligrams, presently one day's dosage for a patient. This makes using this dietary source on a regular basis a daunting task! To make things worse, testosterone taken by mouth, unless it is in a special easily absorbed and stable form, is broken down in the liver and never gets into the general circulation. This makes Pliny's treatment, though it must have sounded like a theoretically good idea at the time, practically useless – apart from the doubtless strong placebo effect.

Later, the Roman physician Aretaeus, who gave the first detailed description of sugar diabetes, wrote:

> *For it is the semen, when possessed of vitality, which makes us to be men, hot, well braced in limbs, well-voiced, spirited, strong to think and act.*

He added the rider that *'for when the semen is not possessed of its vitality, persons become shrivelled'*, which is a good description of the wrinkled skin and wasted muscles of the testosterone deficient male.

The Renaissance

It was only with the wave of radical new thinking that swept through Europe at the end of the fifteenth century that medicine broke free of the bondage imposed on it by Galen's dogma.

This rebirth in both the arts and sciences was precipitated by two events. One was the fall of Constantinople in 1453, which ended the Byzantine Empire and caused many scholars to move to Italy. As a result there was a revival of Greek medical thought in terms of the ideas and observations of Hippocrates.

The other was the information revolution started by the printing of the Gutenberg Bible in 1454, which soon spread to the production of medical texts. Let's hope that the new information revolution produced by the computer and the Internet, which is starting to give us access to medical databases all over the world, will produce even greater advances in freedom of thought on all medical subjects, including the andropause.

One of my heroes from the Renaissance period is Paracelsus (1493–1541), or, to give him his full title, Aureolus Theophrastus Bombastus von Hohenheim.

He was the most important medical thinker of the sixteenth century. As his name suggests, he was a Swiss swashbuckling physician and chemist, who not only had the audacity to challenge Galen's ideas, but publicly burned his books. He revived Hippocratic thought and ideals in medicine and introduced many new ones of his own, especially in relation to thyroid disease. He died unloved and unrecognized by the medical establishment of his day, but left a legacy of original thought which led to fresh medical thinking and experimentation on hormonal factors in health and disease. His approach influenced, among others, Charles Darwin, who appealed to scientists to abandon intellectual 'idolatry'.

Paracelsus introduced a new vision of disease as a distinct explicable entity which could and should be treated. This was in opposition to the Galenic view that most conditions were untreatable and should be borne with fatalistic resignation. Paracelsus successfully introduced mercurials for the treatment of syphilis, for example, the most feared disease of the sixteenth century, which was viewed in the same light as AIDS today. Perhaps we need to invoke the spirit of Paracelsus to encourage a wider discussion of the male menopause.

How did the intelligent public view ageing in the male at that time? With his usual intuitive clinical accuracy, Shakespeare described the seven ages of man in his play *As You Like It*. We can now recognize how each age is influenced by the effects of testosterone:

> *At first the infant,*
> *Mewling and puking in the nurse's arms.*

In the infant there is no real difference between the testosterone levels in boys and girls, though intrauterine differences have left their physical and emotional imprints.

> *And then the whining schoolboy, with his satchel,*
> *And shining morning face, creeping like snail*
> *Unwillingly to school.*

The surge of testosterone at puberty generates the rebellious male nature, as well as the increase in skin oil or sebum, which makes the skin shine and later in excess causes acne. The sexual characteristics of the adult male appear at this stage.

> *And then the lover,*
> *Sighing like furnace, with a woful ballad*
> *Made to his mistress' eyebrow.*

With the libido driven by the peaking levels of testosterone going full blast and rampant priapic power available, mating and nest-building activities normally tend to predominate now.

> *Then a soldier,*
> *Full of strange oaths, and bearded like the pard,*
> *Jealous in honour, sudden and quick in quarrel,*
> *Seeking the bubble reputation*
> *Even in the cannon's mouth.*

Plenty of testosterone still, making him belligerent and driving him through what is often a period of questing and hasty decisions, the 'mid-life crisis'.

> *And then the justice,*
> *In fair round belly with good capon lin'd,*
> *With eyes severe, and beard of formal cut,*
> *Full of wise saws and modern instances;*

With testosterone activity declining, the scene is set for the male menopause to appear, along with the fatty degeneration shared with the capon, showed by weight gain and the muscle deterioration seen first in the Elizabethan couch potato's expanding waistline.

> *The sixth age shifts*
> *Into the lean and slipper'd pantaloon,*
> *With spectacles on nose and pouch on side,*
> *His youthful hose well sav'd a world to wide*
> *For his shrunk shank; and his big manly voice,*
> *Turning again towards childish treble, pipes*
> *And whistles in his sound.*

Now the decreasing free testosterone levels and lack of physical activity fail to maintain muscle mass, particularly in the legs, so that the calves and thighs shrink. Lack of testosterone also results in thinning of the vocal chords, which return to their prepubertal state, giving a higher pitch.

Last scene of all,
    That ends this strange eventful history,

> *Is second childishness, and mere oblivion,*
> *Sans teeth, sans eyes, sans taste, sans everything.*

The old saying that what you don't use you lose comes sadly true at this stage of life. There is considerable evidence to suggest, however, that testosterone treatment can slow the rate of physical and mental deterioration in this final stage, and help men to maintain both the will and ability to continue active life till they drop. You now have the choice!

The Eighteenth and Nineteenth Centuries

The dominant figure in experimental medicine in the eighteenth century was the English surgeon John Hunter (1728–93). Among his amazing range of original studies were the experiments supporting his view that sexual characteristics 'depend on the effects that the ovaria and testicles have upon the constitution'. He obtained evidence for this statement in a variety of ways.

An interesting experiment on how the testes enlarged in the mating season in a variety of animals was carried out by killing and preserving a series of London cock sparrows at monthly intervals from midwinter to spring. Hunter's students later reported his demonstration that:

> *The one killed in December has testes not bigger than a small pin's head, the rest are gradually larger, the testes of the last, killed in April, are as large as the top of your little finger.*[4]

We now know that this seasonal growth of the testes, with the accompanying surge in testosterone, is due to the longer days triggering the pineal gland at the base of the brain to switch off production of its 'hibernation hormone', melatonin. This in turn causes the pituitary gland to produce more of the hormones which rouse the dormant testes to spring fever pitch. It seems, however, that bright city lights are now suppressing this seasonal cycle and causing mating activity in cosmopolitan sparrows all year round. Though in humans there is a slight surge in conception rates around holiday periods such as Christmas, there is a larger rise in late spring and early summer, so we still retain this link between sunshine and sex.

What has not been sufficiently recognized is that Hunter carried out transplantation experiments which showed that if the spur of a hen were transplanted to a cock, it would grow to the size of a cock's spur. He went on to demonstrate that if the small spur of a young cock were transplanted to a hen, it failed to grow at all. Also, in 1771, he transplanted cocks' testicles into their abdomens and observed that they continued to grow there. He transplanted them into the same site in hens, too, with some evidence of a masculinizing effect.

However, Hunter failed to publish his results, illustrating the truth of that old medical dictum 'Publish or perish'. It was not until over 70 years later, in 1849, that a German professor at the University of Göttingen, Adolf Berthold, who knew of Hunter's work, repeated the experiment, showing that capons could grow into normal cocks following testicular transplants:

They crowed quite considerably, often fought among themselves and with other young roosters, and showed a normal inclination to hens.[5]

In particular the transplants prevented shrinkage of the comb, restoring this dramatic red crowning glory which signals the male's sexual maturity. It was clear proof that the testis produced a substance which travelled in the blood to maintain the sexual characteristics of the adult male animal.

This first well documented successful hormone replacement therapy inaugurated a century of attempts to use testicular extracts or implants to rejuvenate men.

However, most of these attempts were either of doubtful effectiveness, mainly relying either on the placebo effect of giving patients a novel form of treatment or on fraudulent confidence tricks based on the instinctive wish for a long and active life. It is difficult to this day to decide whether doctors offering rejuvenation treatments are 'leading edge pioneers' or 'medical buccaneers' who navigate 'this poorly charted sea of medical research'. Time and future research will tell.

One who must certainly be regarded as a pioneer was the eminent neurologist and physiologist Charles Edouard Brown-Séquard (1817–94). He had a distinguished career in France, where he was the successor of the celebrated physiologist Claude Bernard at the Sorbonne in Paris, and held posts in England and America, as well as being the first to demonstrate that the adrenal glands were essential to life.

However, his colleagues became critical of his ideas when in 1869 he suggested that 'the feebleness of old men is in part due to the diminution in function of the testicles' and:

If it were possible to inject, without danger, sperm into the veins of old men, one would be able to obtain with them some manifestations of rejuvenation at once with respect to intellectual work and the physical powers of the organism.[6]

They were even more sceptical when in 1889, still actively researching his ideas at the age of 72, he announced at a learned gathering in Paris that he had mentally and physically rejuvenated himself with subcutaneous injections of extracts of the testicles of dogs and guinea-pigs. Within three weeks the *British Medical Journal* had published a report on his lecture criticizing his ideas and manner of their presentation. Under the heading 'The pentacle of rejuvenescence' it pronounced sarcastically:

The statements he made – which have unfortunately attracted a good deal of attention in the public press – recall the wild imaginings of mediaeval philosophers in search of an elixir vitae.[7]

Similar responses to reports on the benefits of treating the male menopause are still prevalent over 100 years later. Looking back, Brown-Séquard's ghost might well comment, *'Plus ça change, plus c'est la meme chose.'*

In England and the rest of Europe his results were said to be due to autosuggestion, or even hypnosis, which was very fashionable in France at the time. He tried to counteract this notion by not giving the patients any idea of the results he was expecting, though any treatment by such a distinguished and imposing professor must have had some placebo effect.

He also sent his extracts to sympathetic colleagues in England and America. Though some reported good results, the general medical reaction in Britain to what rapidly became known as one type of 'organotherapy', or treatment with glandular extracts or transplants, was hostile. However, some of the critics were given pause for thought by work going on at the same time on the more obvious, reproducible and clear cut benefits of treating thyroid deficient (myxoedematous) patients with thyroid extracts.

In America, on the contrary, reaction to Brown-Séquard's work was over-enthusiastic and the testicular extract was widely inflicted by charlatans on a gullible public as 'the Elixir of Life' for every type of ailment from senility to tuberculosis. This and other organotherapies became even more fashionable because of the simultaneous introduction of 'serotherapies' – the use of sera and vaccines of animal origin for the prevention and treatment of infectious diseases.

The failure of such extracts led to Brown-Séquard dying a discredited man. Moralists were quick to criticize his therapy and the ridicule that it brought to the whole field of research into the hormonal functions of the testis has lasted to the present day. He *'made the blunder that put the male hormone in the scientific dog-house'*, as Paul de Kruif points out.[8]

In Victorian England, matters relating to sexual activity were considered 'not quite nice' and unsuitable topics for research anyway. Even learned and very influential physiologists such as Sir Edward Sharpey-Schafer (1850–1935), who wrote many papers and a book on 'endocrine organs', had a Freudian block about reproductive hormones and in a lecture on 'internal secretions' given to the British Medical Association in London in 1895 denied that the testes had any endocrine actions. It is amazing that so great a pioneer in other areas of endocrinology could have so complete a blind spot.

Another testicular experiment with an unfortunate long-term result was that performed in 1896 by two Austrian doctors who claimed that testicular extracts of bull's testicles could improve the strength of their hand muscles. They concluded: *'The training of athletes offers an opportunity for further research in this area.'* This report foreshadowed the damaging influence of steroid abuse by athletes on the medical and public image of testosterone treatment.

The Twentieth Century

Endocrinology

The twentieth century heralded the birth of the science of hormones, or endocrinology. The word 'hormone' was introduced in 1905 by a British physiologist, Professor Ernest Starling, in a lecture he was giving at the Royal College of Physicians in London. It was derived by two scholarly dons in Cambridge from the Greek verb *hormao*, meaning 'to put into quick motion', 'to excite' or 'to arouse'. Starling used it to describe the 'chemical messengers' that were released into the bloodstream by the body's ductless or endocrine glands (*endon*, 'internal' + *krino*, 'to secrete'), such as the testis, thyroid and adrenals, from the external (*exo*, 'outside') secretions of glands with ducts, the exocrine glands, such as those that produce saliva or tears. The new science lived up to its name by making rapid advances which excited both the public and medical imagination.

Typically the history of any one hormone goes through four stages:

First, there is the observation that a gland or organ produces an internal secretion that has a general effect on the body.

Secondly, methods of detecting the internal secretion and measuring its effects are developed. This is usually initially by biological assay, seeing what action the preparation containing the hormone has on an animal or organ lacking it. Later chemical methods of measurement can be found.

Thirdly, the hormone is extracted from the gland or organ and isolated in a pure form.

Fourthly, chemists define its structure and synthesize it.

Testosterone was the first hormone to be recognized and measured, but because of the complexity of its molecule was relatively slow to be isolated and synthesized.

At the turn of the century, though organotherapy, using extracts of different glands, particularly the thyroid and adrenal, continued to be the subject of much speculation and experimentation, it soon became clear that testicular extracts were not sufficiently powerful to have the effects originally claimed. This was because the minute amount of testosterone produced in the testes is continuously being swept away into the bloodstream and is not stockpiled in the gland.

Remembering the work of Hunter and Berthold, doctors then attempted what would be a difficult feat even today: transplanting testicles from man to man. In 1912 and 1913 two apparently successful operations took place in America. The second of these was performed by a Dr Victor D. Lespinasse of Chicago, who reported full restoration of libido and sexual function over a two-year period in a man previously without desire and impotent from loss of both testes.

The First World War then held up endocrine research and prevented communication between doctors working in different European countries for many years. However, an interesting report emerged that the famous Danish surgeon Thorkild Rovsing had carried out an experiment indicating that testicular function might be important in relation to the circulation, as indeed Brown-Séquard had claimed. After a young soldier had been killed in battle, Rovsing transplanted his testicles into an old man with gangrene, which then, according to the case report, healed completely.

In 1918 the resident physician in San Quentin prison in California, Dr Leo L. Stanley, who had access to many fresh testicles 'donated' by executed prisoners, started transplanting them into other inmates of various ages.

Some of these regained their sexual potency, though how this was measured in the prison is unclear and freedom is a great aphrodisiac. Two years later, because of 'the scarcity of human material', even in that situation, Stanley moved on to transplanting the testes of rams, goats, deer and boars into his rapidly expanding patient population. These testes, perhaps suspiciously, seemed to be equally effective. Interestingly, as with Rovsing, gangrene was among the wide range of conditions from senility to diabetes which Stanley's treatment claimed to benefit.

In the early 1920s, a flamboyant Russian-French surgeon called Serge Voronoff, working in Algiers, made his fame and fortune by transplanting chimpanzee and baboon testicles into humans, and claimed they had powerful rejuvenating effects. This work naturally attracted great medical and public interest, and international deputations of doctors as well as patients from many countries made the pilgrimage to Algiers to investigate Voronoff's 'monkey gland' treatment.

If Voronoff was just fooling people, he did so with a lot of detailed evidence and seemingly convincing results for at least a decade. Even my first professor of physiology at the Middlesex Hospital in London, Samson Wright, described Voronoff's work in detail in his standard textbook of 1926:

> *In successful cases it is claimed that very striking results are obtained from this operation. Old people, with marked signs of senility, are claimed to be thus transformed into vigorous energetic individuals. Previously castrated persons may regain their secondary sex character – e.g. growth of beard and moustache may occur.*[9]

He obviously took this work seriously:

> *While Voronoff's operation appears quite justifiable in young subjects in whom the testes have been damaged or destroyed by injury or disease, the treatment of senility by this method is more questionable. We have no proof whatever that senility is solely due to atrophic changes in the testis; it is almost certain that many other factors are con- cerned. Though the testicular graft may stimulate physical activity and sexual desire, it cannot restore the worn heart, arteries and essential organs to their normal state. There is a grave danger that excessive strain may be put on damaged structures, with disastrous results.*[10]

These same lines of argument are still used today by doctors urging the fatalistic 'do nothing' option.

Pure Testosterone

As the war clouds cleared in Europe after the First World War, a great pharmacological arms race developed with three drug firms competing to be the first to produce the active ingredient of the testicles in pure chemical form. It is an amazing example of synchronicity that after a search for the essence of manhood lasting over 4,000 years, the three different groups passed the finishing post within four months of each other.

First, on 27 May 1935, was Ernst Laqueur, a professor of pharmacology in Amsterdam, who led an excellent research team for the Organon drug company. He emerged triumphant from a veritable mountain of bulls' testicles with a few precious crystals, submitted a paper called '*On crystalline male hormone from testicles*' and coined the name 'testosterone' for it.[11]

Second was a formidable, dynamic German chemist with a duelling scar on his left cheek, Professor Adolf Butenandt. He was working for the Schering Company in Berlin, which had managed to survive the First World War with its manufacturing capacity intact, and in 1923, thanks to hyper-inflation made a profit of 286 million billion marks, after tax, giving the shareholders a dividend of two billion per cent. Some of this profit it invested in collecting 25,000 litres of policemen's urine, enough to fill an Olympic-size swimming-pool. From this, Butenandt, with bravery clearly above and beyond the call of duty, extracted 15 mg, a few crystals, of a relatively inactive urinary breakdown product of testosterone called androsterone.[12]

He then decided that method of preparation was too much like hard work and thought up the much more commercial way by which testosterone is made to this day. He methodically worked out its structure and then produced it, as does the body, from cholesterol, its natural precursor. He sent his paper on this process and the structure of testosterone itself to the *German Journal of Physiological Chemistry* on 24 August 1935.[13]

Just one week later, a Swiss chemical journal received a paper from Leopold Ruzicka, a Yugoslavian chemist working for the Ciba company in Zurich, announcing a patent on the method of production of testosterone from cholesterol.[14] For this work, he and Butenandt received the Nobel Prize in 1939.

Within two years of these momentous discoveries a variety of testosterone preparations were in clinical use. It was soon found that because it was an oily substance which didn't dissolve readily in water, in the pure form it couldn't be absorbed by mouth. So a slow release form that could be given by injection, testosterone propionate, was synthesized and soon became widely used. This proved very successful in patients whose testes were insufficiently active for a variety of reasons, including those showing signs of the male menopause.[15] Rather like insulin injections for diabetics, which had been introduced 15 years earlier, it was dramatically effective in restoring the two big Vs in men's lives: Vitality and Virility. Now that you could 'get it in a bottle', testicular transplants and extracts went out of the window.

Studies on patients throughout the late 1930s and the 1940s showed a wide range of benefits in several serious medical conditions, from heart and circulatory problems, including gangrene, to diabetes.

Though the injections lasted about three days, another form of testosterone was also introduced. Compressed crystals were fused together to form tablets and later small cylindrical pellets which under local anaesthetic could be implanted under the skin of the buttock or abdomen. This was both effective and convenient, as the implant continued to act for six months.[16] Sixty years later this is still one of the best methods of giving long-term testosterone treatment. There are few medical preparations, particularly in endocrinology, which have stood the test of time so well.[17]

A third type of preparation which was also made in the early years of testosterone treatment was a water soluble form called methyl testosterone.[18] Unfortunately, though effective in relieving symptoms, this proved very toxic, especially to the liver. As it was nevertheless widely used for over 50 years and was included in many under the counter gold and silver covered pills claiming almost magical sexual powers, it has done a great deal of harm to the safety image of testosterone. It is amazing that even today, when its dangers have so long been recognized and it has largely been taken off the market throughout the rest of the world, it is still almost the only form of oral testosterone preparation available in the USA, where several safe derivatives cannot be marketed.[19]

Unfortunately, in Britain, this toxic drug is still being manufactured and sold in capsules, also containing the supposed sexual stimulants yohimbine and pemoline, as Prowess. Such toxic products should be banned by international agreement.

Testosterone Used to Treat the Male Menopause

From 1940 onwards, largely because of the obvious improvements brought about by testosterone, it was generally accepted by many doctors that there was a group of symptoms commonly experienced by men in their fifties similar to the female menopause or 'climacteric', from the Greek word *klimacter*, meaning 'the rung of a ladder', and hence a critical period in life at which the vital force begins to decline.

An outstanding paper of this time, which used testosterone as definitive proof of the existence of the male menopause, was published in the prestigious *Journal of the American Medical Association* in 1944. It was called 'The male climacteric: its symptomatology, diagnosis and treatment' and was by two American doctors, Carl G. Heller and Gordon B. Myers.[20] It is well worth looking at this historic paper in detail, as the case has seldom if ever been better made.

The symptoms which the authors attributed to the male climacteric were exactly as described in the next chapter of this book as those of the male menopause: nervousness, depression, impaired memory, the inability to concentrate, easy fatiguability, insomnia, hot flushes, sweating, and loss of libido and potency.

They began by listing all the points raised by those who were sceptical of the existence of this condition and then used their clinical studies to answer them one by one. The majority of these points were based on the general view that no objective evidence had been put forward to prove the menopause was an actual clinical entity, or to differentiate it from neurosis or impotence of purely emotional origin. Also, many men remained fertile to an advanced age and did not show the marked physical changes in body form that menopausal women showed.

To study this, Heller and Myers developed a measure of testicular function based on the hormonal feedback mechanism which controls the production of testosterone in men and oestrogen in women. When the amount of active testosterone or oestrogen drops, the pituitary, the small gland at the base of the brain which is in overall control, releases more of two hormones – gonadotrophins, so called because they stimulate these sex glands. When the activity of the sex hormones increases to the point where they are adequate for the body's needs, the gonadotrophins fall to a low level.

Nowadays gonadotrophins can be measured by sensitive chemical tests on the blood, but in the 1940s Heller and Myers had to extract a 12-hour overnight sample of each man's urine, inject the extract into immature female rats and measure the increase in the weight of their ovaries caused by these hormones. This simple biological test gave surprisingly clear cut results. The urine of normal men, or those whose symptoms were due to anxiety or neurosis, showed virtually no gonadotrophin activity in the urine. Those whose symptoms were due to a true male climacteric syndrome showed high levels of urinary gonadotrophins, as demonstrated by the ovaries of the test rats doubling or trebling in size.

This carefully performed and detailed study gave unequivocal evidence that the male menopause was a physical fact, not just a fiction created by the emotionally disturbed and neurotic. Also, when a therapeutic test was carried out on samples of both groups of men by giving injections of testosterone propionate, the neurotic group 'experienced little, if any, improvement in potency or in well-being'.

By contrast, in the male climacteric group they reported that:

Definite improvement in the symptomatology was noted by the end of the second week in all of the twenty cases treated. Complete abolition of all vasomotor, psychic, constitutional and urinary symptoms was accomplished by the end of the third week in 17 of the 20 cases treated. In the remaining three cases vasomotor and urinary symptoms were abolished but the psychic and constitutional symptoms persisted in spite of continuation of treatment for several months and doubling the dosage for brief periods. It was concluded that these three persons were suffering from involutional melancholia [depression of old age].

The same study also answered a frequent criticism of testosterone treatment which still appears to this day, namely that it will restore libido but not help problems with erections, thus leaving the patient more frustrated than before. Heller and Myers' experience coincides with my own:

> *Sexual potency was restored to normal with these doses in all but 2 cases, in one of which involutional melancholia was present.*

They go on to remark that with increased dosage, *'Sexual vigour in both previously refractory cases exceeded that of normal men.'*

They further gave evidence that this is a real response to testosterone treatment and not just a placebo effect:

> *In 14 cases therapy was subsequently withheld for from four to fourteen weeks and in all instances the symptoms returned and sexual potency was again lost. On resumption of the therapy with testosterone propionate, relief of symptoms was again afforded and sexual potency returned. Thus the specificity of therapy was established.*
>
> *To investigate further the possibility that the improvement may have been due to suggestion, placebo injections were administered. Ampoules containing 1cc of sesame oil, packaged similarly to the original testosterone propionate, were substituted without the patients' knowledge in several cases. No improvement was noted in any case.*

As well as recommending pellet implants for long-term treatment, Heller and Myers made two final important points in this historic paper. These were that *'the male climacteric is not confined to middle and old age but may occur as early as the third decade'* and their conclusion:

> *Whereas in the female the menopause is an invariable and physiologic accompaniment of the ageing process, in the male the climacteric is an infrequent and pathologic accompaniment of the ageing process.*

We will see later why the male menopause may have become more common half a century on and yet is still not being properly diagnosed or treated.

Dr Tiberius Reiter

Starting in 1950, Dr Tiberius Reiter, a German physician who trained in Berlin, Edinburgh and Glasgow but set up in private practice in London's Harley Street, used testosterone pellet implants to treat men in their forties, fifties, sixties and seventies suffering what he called 'IDUT syndrome'.[21,22] These initials indicated the main features of the condition: Impotence, Depression, Urinary disturbances and Thyroid overactivity. Included in the latter were irritability, headaches and attacks of rapid heartbeats, particularly at night, which just about completes the classic picture of the male menopause. Reiter attributed all these symptoms to testosterone deficiency.

Over 20 years he treated more than 350 patients with very good clinical results. These he wrote up in considerable detail in a series of eloquent articles, carefully documenting the improvements in each symptom on his own rating scale. As well as being the first to actually measure lowered testosterone levels in his patients before treatment, he emphasized its safety and suggested that far from being dangerous, it showed evidence of benefiting the heart and prostate gland.[23] He also wrote a monograph describing his method of implanting testosterone pellets into the buttocks for Organon, the company who made the implants.[24] These are the method and materials I use to this day in some cases for long-term testosterone treatment, and it is still a powerful, safe and effective way of giving the hormone.

On speaking to his medical colleagues, several of his patients and his widow Nancy Reiter, an interesting picture emerges of this remarkable man. He was a dynamic, charismatic individual who delighted in the improvements he saw in his patients. He believed in a broad approach to treatment and would sometimes take his patients to his favourite fish restaurant to teach them at a pleasant practical level the benefits to virility of eating oysters, with their high zinc content. As Nancy put it, he was regarded with *'plenty of scepticism from the medical world – but the patients kept coming!'*

Reiter was well received in America, where he published three articles in the *Journal of the American Geriatrics Society* between 1963 and 1965. In 1965 he also lectured at their 22nd Annual Meeting in New York City, receiving considerable interest and approval.

However, in Britain he remained an unrecognized prophet. Despairing of getting his message across, he devised a cunning plan. He went to a meeting on endocrinology at the prestigious Royal Society of Medicine, the heart of the medical establishment, in Wimpole Street, London, and at the question time at the end, stood up to deliver a long fiery diatribe about the virtues of testosterone treatment. When the chairman finally managed to shut him up – which took some doing – he went to the front entrance of the imposing building and met a group of journalists he had previously summoned. He then gave them full details of his learned address to the Royal Society, which were duly printed, together with his picture, in the newspapers that evening.

Perhaps not surprisingly, such direct action did not endear Reiter to academic doctors, but he died much loved by his patients in 1972, truly another hero of the hormonal revolution.

Dr Jens Møller

Another of the great pioneers of testosterone treatment was the Danish doctor Jens Møller. With all the fire and tenacity of his Viking ancestors he fought a 30-year war for its use against the medical establishment in Denmark and throughout Europe. I had the privilege of working with him during the last 10 years of that war and it was he who in 1977 first interested me in testosterone.

At the time I had been working as Senior Lecturer in Chemical Pathology at St Mary's Hospital Medical School in London. Though my office and research laboratory were located within the department of Professor Vivian James, one of the world's leading researchers on steroid biochemistry, which includes the study of testosterone, oestrogens, cortisol and other related hormones, I was more excited by the stress hormones such as adrenaline and noradrenaline which appeared more directly related to stress, tension and heart disease, my main area of research activity.

However I was very much interested in exercise as a means of balancing the effects of stress and protecting the heart from them. As part of this programme of research, I was taking part in a study set up by the Medical Research Council at the City Gymnasium at Moorgate. The founder and owner of this gymnasium was an ex-Olympic weight-lifting coach called Alistair Murray. With tremendous energy and enthusiasm, he originated the use of vigorous but not violent exercise in the form of circuit training in both the prevention and treatment of heart disease in London businessmen. We had just written a book together for the British Sports Council called *F40: Fitness on Forty Minutes a Week*,[25] based on his ideas and reporting this research.

One day while I was at the gym Alistair called me into

his office to meet a tall Dane with what I thought was a tall story. Though friendly, this doctor had a military bearing and the charm of a diplomat which he could switch on or off at will. When it was off he could be what he described as *'very direct'*. He was then in his seventies, though with the brisk manner and energy of a man 20 years younger. As I learned later, he had had a varied career demonstrating the power of testosterone treatment to excite extreme passions – in the minds of medical men.

Born in North Jutland in 1904, Møller left home at the age of 16 and became a successful entrepreneur, working in turn in Paris, London and Berlin. Even with money to burn, however, he found his business career meaningless and at the end of the Second World War enrolled at the university medical school in Copenhagen, getting his entry qualifications in three months rather than the usual year. He qualified five years later, at the age of 50, and began his medical career, which was to be as unusual and turbulent as his previous one in business.

After a variety of work in hospitals and the pharmaceutical industry, he decided he wanted to be a neurosurgeon and worked in Sweden for a time. As neurosurgical jobs were few and far between, he took a locum job with a private physician working in Copenhagen, a decision which was to alter the course of the rest of his career.

Doctor Tvedegaard, whose name I shall abbreviate to Dr T. as he was already a controversial figure in Danish medicine because of his use of testosterone, used the hormone to treat severe arterial disease, particularly in the legs. He had studied its use by German doctors and seen amazing results even in the most severe cases of gangrene.

The typical history given by his patients was one of painful cramps in the calves of the legs on walking, especially uphill on cold days, a condition known as 'intermittent claudication'. As the blood supply became worse, this gradually progressed to more continuous pain, even at rest and in bed at night, so that the patient would have to hang his leg out of bed to ease the intense discomfort. Eventually the limb would stay cold and blue most of the time, and an otherwise trivial injury to the foot would turn into an infection leading to gangrene of one or more toes. According to conventional practice at the time, these would then have to be amputated and the surgeons would start on what often turned out to be a series of amputations, nibbling their way up one or both legs to above the knee.

Testosterone injections, often in considerably higher doses than generally prescribed, seemed to have halted or in some cases even reversed the otherwise inexorable process at almost any stage. Walking would be prolonged because the cramps in the calves would come on later and later, and even disappear, leaving a very happy wanderer. Night cramps would also go, which greatly improved the quality of sleep. Cold, blue, painful feet and legs would become pink and comfortable as the circulation mysteriously improved. Even gangrene would heal without surgical intervention, much to the relief and delight of the patients and their relatives. Though this did not necessarily prolong their lives indefinitely, it did give them a much better quality of life and could prevent them becoming crippled by their circulatory problems. Many were the patients who went happier to their graves with two whole legs rather than one or none as a result of this testosterone treatment.

At the time this was very strange and inexplicable. However, even more curious was that instead of other doctors becoming interested in this treatment, investigating it further in an open-minded spirit of scientific enquiry and perhaps even trying it on some of their more severe cases, who after all had nothing to lose except their legs, the reverse occurred. Because testosterone treatment did not fit the medical orthodoxy of the time, was not recognized in the groves of academia and was a dirty foreign product originating in still deeply detested Germany of all places, Danish doctors closed ranks and minds against it. It seemed that the rigid, doctrinal, Galenic attitude had once again triumphed over the investigative, clinical, Hippocratic one.

Though burning at the stake (other than intellectually) had rather gone out of fashion, doctors still managed to find ways of dealing with troublesome medical heretics. Suppressing their ideas by turning down their papers for medical meetings and publications was a good start. If theories are not published or discussed, they can't be any good, can they? Unsurprisingly, Dr T.'s three papers for Danish medical journals were rejected.

Dr T. was often outspoken and critical of his colleagues' attitude and made many enemies among them. So when an opportunity for discrediting him presented itself, it was eagerly seized.

In Denmark at that time the law relating to medicines said that conditions could only be treated with the drugs officially recognized as being effective in those disorders. Because of prevailing medical opinion, not only in Denmark but in most other countries as well, testosterone was not on the list of drugs to be used for circulatory problems. Even if an army of 1,000 people whose limbs had been saved marched up and down outside the Danish Parliament for a week, the law was the law, and medical opinion could not be moved to change it for sweet reason's sake.

Also, patients could have some of the costs of certain 'vital medicines' refunded, provided the condition for which they were given was on the authorized list and the prescriptions were written on the appropriate red forms. Dr T.'s deeply held view was that testosterone was a literally life-saving 'vital medicine' and, because it came mainly from the testes, he found a category of 'genital insufficiency' which he thought qualified its use in the cases he saw and daily wrote his prescriptions on red forms.

Unfortunately, in August 1957 this came to the notice of Danish Health Service officials, who 'saw red' and reacted in a surprisingly dramatic fashion. Rather than take the case up through the usual medical disciplinary channels, they sent the state police round the same day to officially charge Dr T. and Dr Møller with betraying the Government for money, because testosterone was not a 'vital medicine'.

This rapidly escalated into a very public *cause célèbre* with many court hearings. Questions were asked in the Danish Parliament. Dr T.'s health soon deteriorated under the strain, so Dr Møller, who was made of sterner stuff, was left holding the testosterone baby.

Undeterred by rulings against them in the courts, he mobilized public opinion in their favour. He did a detailed study of the literature and went to Germany to discuss the use of testosterone with the leading endocrinologists of the day, who were very supportive of his ideas. He then organized a public meeting of over 1,500 patients and relatives to raise funds for the fight. He lined up doctors from the health authority in the front row, deluged them with this new scientific evidence and then said, *'Contradict me if you can.'* They couldn't, and left the hall in a state of confusion and acute embarrassment.

The fight then got very dirty. The police tried to seize all the patients' case notes and deprive the defendants of their evidence. Dr Møller took the case notes home and piled them in the fireplace, telling his wife to set fire to them if the police called while he was out. The prosecution even made up stories from patients about how they had been treated. Fortunately, many grateful and influential patients kept up the legal battle. Literally their lives and limbs depended on it.

Finally, after two years, a Minister of Justice who was on the State Medical Ethics Committee and had a close relative who had been greatly helped by Dr Møller's treatment got the court's decision reversed and the case called off. Not only that, but the Director of the Danish Health Authority, who had been one of Dr Møller's fiercest opponents, saw the effects of the treatment on his family and friends, and changed his mind to the extent that he became Director of LBK, an organization which was set up to promote the use of testosterone.

The facts in this amazing case are documented in a book called *The Tvedegaard – Møller Trial: A fight against injustice* written a year later by another Danish doctor who had supported their cause.[26]

Though the medical establishment in Denmark generally remained hostile to the 'Dr Tvedegaard treatment', which they used to tell their students was *'hormonal humbug'*, Dr Møller's practice flourished. He used to see 50 or more patients a day and sometimes they had to queue in the street outside his clinic in the fashionable Store Kongensgade (Great King Street).

As is traditional with native prophets, Dr Møller began to receive much more recognition from abroad than in his own country. Many distinguished doctors from America, Britain and all over Europe visited his clinic, but Danish medics seldom came to call except when they wanted research funds from Møller's rapidly growing charitable foundations.

Not unnaturally, these experiences left Dr Møller feeling somewhat paranoid, and it became his mission for the rest of his life to hammer home the message of the effectiveness and safety of testosterone. To this end he established the European Organization for the Control of Circulatory Diseases, or EOCCD, at a meeting of the European Parliament in Strasbourg in 1976 and enlisted many prominent politicians as well as doctors in his fight against what he called '*the international enemy*' of circulatory problems.

From 1977 onwards I made many visits to his clinic in Copenhagen and saw for myself the dramatic benefits of testosterone treatment to the circulation, especially in the legs. I came to realize how testosterone had its effects and helped Dr Møller to edit the books he was writing.[27,28,29]

Also I went with him as he charged round Europe in his capacity of President of the EOCCD, holding meetings in London, Luxembourg, Strasbourg, Bonn, Berlin and Munich. We visited many eminent authorities throughout Europe and Dr Møller achieved a great deal of scientific support for his ideas. It was difficult to keep up with him even when he entered his eighties and it soon became apparent that he certainly took his own medicine, which was as effective for him as it was for his patients.

When he finally died in 1989, active to the last, he left thriving national and international organizations which are carrying on his work under the direction of his able young successor, Dr Michael Hansen. This seems a fitting guarantee that Dr Jens Møller's heroic work in the service of testosterone will continue to bear fruit.

This brings the testosterone story almost up to the present day. My own experiences in trying to prove the existence of the male menopause have closely mirrored those of many of the characters featured in this story, particularly Paul de Kruif, Dr Tiberius Reiter and Dr Jens Møller. Attempts to debate the condition and its treatment with other doctors, especially those in related specialities such as endocrinology and urology, have met more with what could best be described as blatantly illogical denial. This has been laced with emotion and rhetoric far exceeding the spirit of detached scientific debate. Interestingly, the family doctors with whom I have had the opportunity of discussing the subject, both individually and in teaching seminars, have been much more enquiring and open-minded in their response than the specialists.

It seems that history is likely to repeat itself, as it often does, and that testosterone replacement therapy for men will arrive by the same route as oestrogen replacement therapy for women. It was the enthusiasm of the women themselves which gathered converts to the cause, not the recommendations of doctors. Only after several years of intense opposition, including predictions of doom and disaster from the majority of gynaecologists, did doctors generally become supportive of those seeking treatment. The situation has now changed to the point where the majority are in favour and a few have become downright evangelical – while still remaining generally hostile to the idea of similar treatment for men!

A recent poll in a major British national newspaper established that 97 per cent of its readers believed that the male menopause was a fact and should be treated. However, in the same month at a meeting of urological specialists at St Bartholomew's Hospital in London, only one third agreed the condition existed and even fewer considered treatment might be safe or effective.

So that you can better make up your own mind on whether this is a fictitious condition or a real one which should be treated, let's now look at the experiences of some of the thousand or so patients I have seen over the last 20 years with symptoms they put down to the male menopause and the benefits they received from testosterone treatment.

Chapter Two

The Male Menopause or Andropause

What's in a name? Well, in the case of the male menopause, a lot. It is probably one of the main reasons why the condition has failed to achieve the recognition it deserves.

For the sake of clarity and brevity, and to ease acceptance by both the general public and the medical establishment (who already recognize the name, if not the disorder), from now on I will mainly use the term 'andropause' when referring to this condition in men and 'menopause' when referring to the equivalent condition in women.

After all, the term 'menopause' was introduced by French doctors in the 1870s, combining two Greek words – *menses* ('periods') and *pausis* ('stop') – to indicate the time in a woman's life when the monthly periods stop, just as the word 'menarche', combining *menses* ('periods') and *arkhe* ('start'), means their beginning. When applied to men, the word is therefore both inaccurate and, because of its effeminate overtones, somewhat derogatory. One of the aims of this book is to change that image and make the whole subject easier for men to talk about and think about.

'Andropause' combines two Greek words – *andro* ('male') and *pausis* ('stop') – and means 'when masculinity ceases', which is a much more accurate description of the condition. It is doubly appropriate because the root of the problem is an inadequate supply of androgens, the hormones which provide manliness (*andro*, 'male', *gen*, 'give'), and which can be used as an effective remedy for the problem.

Women are used to visiting their gynaecologist – *gynaeco* ('female'), *logist* (scientist) – to sort out their problems. I suggest that men should be equally willing to consult their 'andrologists'. These practitioners are beginning to have an expanding role outside that of male fertility to include the particular health concerns of men and are now in a good situation to advise on testosterone replacement therapy to treat the andropause.[1]

Let's start with a brief sketch of the condition, how it begins and how we can recognize it happening to us or those around us. Its often insidious onset can be at any time from the age of 30 onwards, though typically it is in the fifties. One of the reasons it's often missed is that it is usually more gradual in onset than the menopause in the female, although it is more severe in its long-term consequences. It is a crisis of vitality just as much as virility, even though its most obvious sign is loss both of interest in sex and of erectile power. This change is surprisingly often overlooked or ignored, either because the man is so pressurized by the rest of his life that he assumes it is an inevitable part of growing older or because his sexual partner has lost interest as well.

Besides lack of sex drive, there is often loss of drive in professional or business life, so that the leader becomes the led, the tiger becomes the sheep.

There is also often fatigue, lethargy, exhaustion and

depression, with a sense of hopelessness and helplessness. All too often men change their jobs or their women – anything to ease the malaise they feel – usually with little relief. Sometimes things are made much worse because of the additional stress these changes bring.

Physically, there is often stiffness and pain in the muscles and joints or symptoms of gout and a rapidly deteriorating level of fitness. There may also be signs of accelerated ageing of the heart and circulation.

Typical of the andropause case history is that of John:

I'm just 50 now and I've been very successful in my family's retail business. Because of the recession it is harder to make a living than it was, and work is stressful and not much fun.

My health has always been pretty good, except for one attack of prostatitis associated with a urinary infection five years ago. This 'non-specific urethritis', as they called it, had me up peeing five to ten times a night till it was treated with a four-month long course of antibiotics, but it seemed to clear up completely.

After that, however, though I loved my wife and we had a good life together, with four delightful children, my libido just faded away to nothing compared to the healthy sexual appetite I had for our previous 25 years of happy married life. I've never been one to have affairs, but then I wasn't even interested in 'window-shopping'. I just felt cocooned and detached from even the prettiest girls, as though I just wasn't in the same world as them!

My erections weren't great either, and I had more and more failures in that department, especially when I was tired or had had a few drinks. Morning erections were few and far between, and my wife isn't really turned on at that time. Sex between us was down from two to three times a week to once a month, especially as I didn't like to go into battle if I wasn't sure my guns would fire. In some ways I didn't miss sex all that much, though my wife did, just as you don't miss food if your appetite has gone.

Worse still, I completely lost my drive and ambition over those five years. When I got up in the morning, I felt 'energyless' and completely lethargic, and instead of looking forward to the day, I just wondered what time I could get back to bed. I was really envious of older people with more energy than me. I wasn't giving much time to my wife or the children, which made me feel guilty about them, especially as I was usually as scratchy as a bear with a sore head, and that's not like me.

There were physical changes in me, too. My feet and ankles, knees and back were very stiff in the mornings, which made me feel old and decrepit, and even less like getting out of bed. Often the bed was wringing wet in the mornings because I sweated a lot more than I used to and sometimes this was so bad that my wife had to change the sheets. I found that I flushed easily when the room was warm, but that my feet and hands were cold most of the time. What with that, the night sweats and the lack of sex, my wife was threatening me with single beds!

I don't go to my doctor often, but a year or so ago I went to see him, feeling thoroughly depressed and convinced that something must be wrong with me. He's a good fellow and heard me out sympathetically. But when I said that I thought that my symptoms were just like my wife had had before she went on hormone replacement therapy and wasn't there something similar he could give me, he nearly threw me out of the surgery! I was told to forget it and given a choice of anti-depressants or marriage guidance counselling, or both, but I didn't feel either of these were right for me.

Just as I was getting desperate, my wife saw an article in a magazine about the male menopause being a real condition that could be positively identified and safely treated with testosterone. She said the case described was an exact picture of me. I went through the appropriate tests and safety checks, and started on testosterone capsules by mouth. Within two weeks the symptoms had improved and within a month they had gone. My marriage, my family life and my business have all benefited. I feel like I did

10 years ago. My wife and I would like to know why did I have to have all those wasted unhappy years when my hormone deficiency could have been detected and put right so easily. It seems a reasonable question to ask.

I spend a lot of time going over men's case histories the first time they come to my consulting room and they mainly tend to be variations on the same theme. No one symptom is essential, but the picture is consistent enough to usually be able to make the diagnosis even before examining the patient or doing the detailed blood tests.

Based on the histories of over 1,000 men who have been to see me over the past 10 years and a detailed analysis of the symptoms shown by the first 400 of these, I have built up an 'identikit picture' of the andropausal male. See if it fits anyone you know.

The main complaints can be described as being either mental, such as fatigue, depression, irritability and reduced libido, or physical, such as ageing, aches and pains, sweating and flushing, and failing sexual performance. You can see how close the comparison with the menopause in women.

Let's consider these symptoms one by one in more detail so that you can recognize the andropause when you see it coming. Above all, remember it is usually treatable and, as it says on the front cover of Douglas Adams' *Hitch-hiker's Guide to the Galaxy*, 'Don't Panic!'

Fatigue

Fatigue is the main expression of the loss of overall vitality which characterizes the andropause. In my first series of 400 men it was present in over 80 per cent of cases. It's as though the man's get up and go has got up and gone. This is hardly surprising if you look on the andropause as a hormone deficient state. Remember the word 'hormone' comes from the Greek for 'setting in motion'.

The patients describe this drop in energy levels and its return on treatment very graphically, as in Bruce's case:

Fifty was a turning point for me. Till then I had been pretty active as an advertising executive, but at that time I just seemed to grind to a halt. I felt tired at work, couldn't concentrate, lost my competitive edge and found my job more and more difficult. Partly this was because I was getting more and more short tempered, and I started drinking fairly heavily in the evenings.

At home, I wasn't exactly a bundle of fun either, falling asleep on the sofa every evening. Though everyone told me I needed a good holiday, I was so tired and negative, the interest and energy needed to organize one just didn't seem to be there. My libido had dropped to the point where even a 'Saturday night special' was usually too much trouble, especially as my erections let me down increasingly often. This was all very depressing, especially when a close friend about my age suddenly died of a heart attack.

After having had these symptoms for four years, my marriage was falling apart and I seemed likely to lose my job. Then I read an article in a magazine and felt the author was writing about me, he described my symptoms so exactly. It all seemed so unfair as there wasn't anything in my medical history that I felt was relevant and my family doctor had told me that I had nothing but a touch of depression. However the tests clearly showed a low 'free testosterone' and I started straightaway on capsules to boost levels of the hormone.

The results were dramatic. Within a month I felt as though the treatment had lifted a veil over my life, and I felt generally more vibrant and more virile. After three months my performance at work was back up to speed again and in managerial jargon I was more 'pro-active'. Also, both at home and at work I was rated 'Mr Nice Guy'. My sex life has improved and my wife is delighted with the results of treatment. Things are going well across the board and, feeling more positive about myself and life in general, I have got on top of the alcohol problem, just having a moderate amount of wine at home over the weekend and none during the week.

Conventional female wisdom has it that it is not the man in your life that matters, so much as the life in your man. What is the life in your man? It is the testosterone drive. This is probably the most important force underlying both mental and physical energy. The ability to reproduce by sexual activity is the essential biological function of all animals, the biological imperative, subordinate only to the needs of staying alive long enough to do it and ensure survival of the offspring.

Many and varied are the ritual tests of manhood. Full-scale battles and individual combat for love, honour and leadership are as old as mankind itself. In Germany ritual duelling with swords, inflicting facial scarring, was fashionable before the Second World War. In Spain, young men still show their bravery and impress the girls by running in front of the bulls in the streets of Pamplona. Triumphant racing-drivers worldwide enjoy the heady symbolism of spraying champagne over adoring crowds. In America, depending on the amount of money available (which is a form of financial testosterone), you arm wrestle, play 'chicken' by riding motor-cycles at other young men down the middle of the road or drive your Ferrari Testarossa as fast and as dangerously as you can. Either way hormones have the last word, often literally.

Testosterone, then, is what drives men on for a large part of their lives and, along with intelligence, is often the deciding factor in their social and sexual history. It can be thought of as the 'success hormone'. When a man is winning life's battles it is high and when he's losing it falls. When it gives out on him, and his drive in both bedroom and boardroom fades, he goes onto 'emergency power' and cuts down on all non-essential activity. At home, sex goes out of the window and both social and domestic activities dwindle and die away. All this sets up enormous tensions and resentments within the entire family. The worsening cycle of failures and recrimination tends to disturb sleep and is made worse by the 'ride of the night-time naggers', with the wife keeping the husband awake by reciting his escalating list of errors of omission and commission.

After a bad night, the man goes to work feeling 'lower than a snake's belly', drained of energy and enthusiasm, and tries to get some by drinking endless cups of coffee. These may just make him more nervous and twitchy and raise his anxiety levels even higher. His attention span and ability to concentrate also deteriorate, as does his memory. Not only is he unable to think up new ideas or put them into action, but his ability to sell himself and his projects also slumps.

Unfortunately customers and competitors alike have an unerring ability to spot when a man is down and out of testosterone, even when he is trying his hardest to put on a brave face. Body language can give clues – does the man slouch in with an apologetic, round-shouldered, crouching look or stride in, standing tall, shoulders back, arms outstretched, looking and feeling great? Is his voice high-pitched and wavering and anxious or low-pitched and steady? Pheromones, those airborne hormones derived from the sex hormones and given off by the skin all over the body, but particularly the genitals and armpits, may also give the game away. They can either send out the sweet smell of success or the sour scent of failure.

One famous captain of industry in Britain, Sir John Harvey-Jones, when prodded in the midriff with a pocket tape-recorder by an American lady writer, Gail Sheehy, researching the subject of the male menopause, urbanely replied that he felt sure there was such a condition. He said he had often seen previously dynamic, hard-driving, successful managers *'go off the boil'*, as he put it, sometimes with disastrous consequences for them or their organizations.

Indeed, he felt had been through one such 'fallow period' in his own career about the age of 50, but had fortunately come through it spontaneously. He went on to suggest that the careers of men who ran into such problems could often be saved, with great benefits to the companies for which they worked, if ways could be found to help them through such difficult times.

All too often, however, in a period of recession, the opportunity is taken to fire the andropausal man whose performance is dropping without inquiring, or him admitting, the reason why. To make the situation worse, this frequently happens at the same time as the man is 'fired' from the marriage bed for underachieving at home as well.

Depression

Variously described by the patients as 'negative' or 'low' mood, depression is one of the commonest features of the andropause and in my first series of patients was present in 70 per cent of cases.

Though only rated as mild to moderate on one of the standard psychiatric rating scales used in the study, it was one of the most difficult of the symptoms for the men and their families to live with. After all, together with life and liberty, the pursuit of happiness is written into the American constitution, and most of the patients didn't feel up to pursuing anything, especially happiness.

Typical of their stories is that of Colin:

Eight years ago the bottom dropped out of the stock market and my life at the same time. First my investments went, then my beautiful country home and finally my job as a promoter. There were plenty of reasons to be depressed, but I felt sure I had something more than just a natural reaction to all these problems. My brain felt full of what I can only describe as toxic sludge. I couldn't focus on anything and was very irritable, as well as being tired and weepy.

Going along with my doctor's view that it was just plain depression, I went to see a psychiatrist who tried polypharmacy with every anti-depressant under the sun, including Prozac, but without success. As a hopeless case, I was threatened with electro-convulsive therapy, but protested and was let off with psychotherapy, which got me into tears and then anger in a big way.

Just when I'd given up hope, there was an article in a magazine which talked about hormonally based depression in the 'male menopause'. A light went on in my head when I read how the combination of the vasectomy 20 years ago, when I was just 30, and the large amounts of alcohol taken to blunt the pain of my financial ruin might have made my depression very much longer and more severe by affecting my testosterone levels.

My doctor was fortunately open-minded enough to encourage me to take the tests and they showed twice the usual level of a binding protein in the blood which, as he explained it, was 'tying up' my testosterone so very little of it was active.

On the hormone treatment, the depression gradually lifted over three or four months. Six months later, my energy and drive have doubled, and I'm employable again now. I still occasionally suffer bouts of depression, but they are much shallower and quicker to recede. I'm back on an even keel again much more rapidly now and looking forward to life being plain sailing again after the terrible storm which nearly sank me.

Depression can be very destructive. It can make a man even less optimistic at work and less likely to suggest, start or carry through new projects. At home, it can not only cast a black cloud over the whole house, but also narrow the social horizons. This can continue to the point where the andropausal man never goes out to visit family or friends, who soon get the message that he doesn't want to see them. He is usually to be found slumped in front of the television in a torpid heap. All this causes the social support inside and outside the family to fall away.

Nervousness, anxiety about everything and everybody, and lack of self-confidence often go hand in hand with the depression, as was recognized in studies of the 'male climacteric' 50 years ago. It can also be accompanied by sleep problems, both in getting off to sleep because of intrusive thoughts and worries and in the early waking characteristic of depression. Unfortunately sleeping pills may just worsen the tiredness during the day and contribute to erectile problems at night.

Though after years of depression a man may reach the point where he feels tired of life, fortunately he often doesn't even have enough energy for suicide!

Sometimes it is difficult to tell which came first, the depression or the other symptoms, since if you are severely depressed, tiredness and loss of libido and potency can result. However, only in a very small proportion of my cases was the depression severe enough to account for the other symptoms.

Most of these cases had already been treated with anti-depressants without improvement – some had even got worse. This is because anti-depressants can make feelings of tiredness worse and the majority seem to interfere with erections (though fortunately, there are exceptions, *see pages 176–7*). Personally, I don't usually use any anti-depressants until testosterone treatment has been tried on its own for three to six months, unless the depression is exceptionally severe and life, job or marriage threatening. This is because my original ratings showed, and my consistent experience is, that TRT on its own gently but firmly lifts the depression, often completely, at the same time as it relieves the other andropausal symptoms.

Irritability

One of the most distressing symptoms of the andropause, both for the men suffering from it and their families, is irritability. This can be entirely unusual for the person concerned or an even shorter fuse in somebody with an already low flash point.

Trivial issues will irritate the man as much if not more than important ones. At work, the firm starts to recruit nothing but idiots, then trains them to work against him and there are no dirty tricks they won't try. At home the whole family deliberately tries to annoy him and succeeds brilliantly! They do all the wrong things at all the wrong times in all the wrong ways. Without having to try he gets into endless arguments with them and ends up infuriated, his patience, like the rest of him, utterly exhausted. He may well be aware that he is being unreasonable and be ashamed of it, but still be unable to do anything about it.

Bernard describes this well:

I suppose it all began when I contracted mumps at the age of 26. This was one of the most serious illnesses I had experienced. My testicles became swollen, so much so I could hardly walk. I had to wear a support just to go to the toilet. Every footstep was agony. I also lost a couple of days. I was delirious and remember very little. Three to four weeks later I was almost back to normal, although one testicle was smaller than the other. Nothing seemed to have been adversely affected and, whilst not ravenous, my sexual appetite seemed normal.

Several years later, around the age of 40, I seemed to be experiencing a number of things. First and foremost I was irritable, irrationally moody and intolerant of other people. The supermarket checkout was constructed just to annoy me. The shop assistant was an idiot and out to obstruct me. The other car driver was a moron and should never have been given a licence. They were all trying to cut me up, hinder me and generally make life difficult for me. I invented both 'trolley rage' and 'road rage'!

On top of this my sexual appetite was zero and erections often failed me. My wife by this time was convinced I was having an affair. It all added up – no sex and an attitude to boot! Finally my wife gave me the ultimatum: see a doctor or we split. A week later I had an interview and a blood test which confirmed a hormone deficiency and that treatment would be appropriate. I was prescribed a course of testosterone capsules which I started immediately.

Ten days later I was a changed man. I felt a tremendous burden had been taken from me. I felt energetic, I became more assertive and I had regained my sexual appetite. My job became easier, I made decisions more easily and I had the energy and determination to see things through. I felt more optimistic and no longer had this feeling of frailty or vulnerability. My erection was much stronger and didn't fail me at the crucial moment. My attitude changed, I returned to being the laid-back, happy and contented person I had been. No more anger, no more moods. I could now enjoy life instead of feeling angry as it passed me by.

Six years later I'm still on the treatment. My job hasn't changed very much but I can handle it much more easily and confidently. I am more successful at doing what is needed. I've gained a lot of self-confidence and I'm not at all susceptible to bouts of depression. My family life is very much happier and the relationship between myself and my stepson has moved *much further forward. My wife and I have regained our loving relationship and our sex life is much more satisfactory to us both.*

Time and again stories like this completely go against the idea of testosterone being the hormone responsible for male aggression and violent behaviour. Usually what is often described all too literally as 'impotent rage' is associated with *low* levels of testosterone activity. When they are restored to normal by treatment the man feels more confident and assertive, and this doesn't seem to overshoot into aggression.

At home, however, the family may have got used to having a human doormat around, and the marked change may not always be welcome as the new man puts his foot down with a firm hand.

Reduced Libido

The word 'libido' means sex drive or sexual appetite and is the same word in Latin, where it was taken to mean 'desire' or 'lust'. One thing that men and women have in common is that their level of libido at any one time is governed by the higher centres in the brain and conditioned by life experience, social factors and hormones, principally testosterone.

This is surprising, since men normally have about 20 times the testosterone level of women, but though men may set the ball rolling more often, most couples end up with a fair measure of agreement about a happy level of sexual activity between them. Extreme exceptions such as when a man is a multiple rapist or a misogynist, or a woman a nymphomaniac or totally frigid throughout her life, are nearly always due to psychological causes rather than hormonal ones.

However, because the baseline level is so much lower

in women, relatively small variations of testosterone may cause big swings in libido. For example, at the middle of the menstrual cycle, when the woman is ovulating and at her most fertile, there is a surge in her testosterone level to put her in the mood for sex.[2] Women who are more assertive and take up more traditionally masculine roles in society such as lawyers[3,4] or business bosses have been found to have higher testosterone levels and frequently are sexually more active.[5] In the USA complaints of sexual harassment of male employees by their female bosses, unheard of a few years ago, are becoming relatively commonplace.

Though the factors affecting libido are complex (for more information, see the series of books *The Disorders of Sexual Desire* by the American sexologist, Dr Helen Singer Caplan), many women with low libido, particularly around the time of the menopause, can be helped by carefully administered low dosage testosterone. If the dose is excessive, not only may masculinizing effects such as increased facial hair and enlargement of the clitoris occur, but the libido may become excessive. The Australian feminist Germane Greer described on a television programme how she was put in an embarrassing situation when a doctor gave her too much of a long-acting testosterone compound and she suddenly found out *'what a rapist felt like'*. This had the unfortunate effect of being one of the factors which turned her against the use of HRT in women, as argued in her book *The Change.*[6]

In the States, a group of women who call themselves 'The Third Sex' deliberately take high doses of testosterone. Despite having to shave hair all over their body frequently and getting shrinkage of their breasts, they reckon that the overall buzz they get from it, and the almost insatiable sexual appetite that goes with clitoral enlargement, makes it worth the chemical sex change.

With the andropause, one of the commonest complaints, present in 80 per cent of cases, is a reduction in libido. This usually comes on gradually over a period of months or years, as the level of active testosterone wanes. If the onset is sudden, or related to a particular event such as illness, the arrival of the first child in the family or the discovery that the partner is having an affair, a physical or emotional cause is suggested rather than a hormonal change. However in extreme cases one can lead to the other.

The fall in libido affects every aspect of a man's sex life, reducing the frequency of sexual thoughts, fantasies and even dreams. The number of times he feels in the mood for sex goes down and the partner may be convinced, usually entirely wrongly, that he has gone right off them, is having an affair, or both. This can often cause problems in the relationship, which further saps the libido, because it can be difficult to be sexually turned on by an angry partner.

In nearly half the cases, the partner's libido then joins the downward spiralling of desire. The 'chemistry of charisma' seems to dictate that as a man's desire decreases, so does his desirability. So then neither party thinks it worthwhile to seek help.

In the most extreme cases, even the most beautiful, attractive or available of sexual partners fails to raise the slightest sexual interest. What Noël Coward called that *'sly biological urge'*, is no longer working and his song of *'Let's do it'* becomes *'I won't dance – don't ask me'*.

Reduced Potency

Reduced potency, in terms of obtaining or maintaining an erection, is one of the most distressing symptoms of the andropause and occurs in about 80 per cent of cases. The word 'potent' comes from the same Latin word meaning 'to have power, strength, ability or authority' or 'to be able to achieve the sexual penetration of a woman and to father children'. So a potentate is a ruler or a monarch who leads any group or endeavour, and has the power and position to rule over others. In many Eastern countries it is traditionally accepted that a ruler can have many wives or mistresses to demonstrate his position of dominance. When it becomes known that his sexual vigour is falling, his fall from power soon follows.

So, with potency seemingly the very essence of masculinity, its lack usually makes the sufferer feel much less of a man in all areas of his life. He is often more ashamed of this than any other symptom. And just using the modern medical parlance of 'erectile dysfunction' doesn't help a lot when the blunt fact of the matter is that in all senses of the term you can't get it up or keep it up, and you feel down about it!

The onset of erection problems is usually gradual and often starts insidiously with fewer early morning spontaneous erections, or 'morning glories' as some people call them. As the comedian Robin Williams, who himself looks like a regular high testosterone 'High-T Guy', quipped in a recent stage show at the Metropolitan Opera House in New York, the penis is usually up and on parade five minutes before you are in the mornings. Indeed, it can be compared to a stand-up comedian who if he has a few bad shows, and worse still gets booed by the audience, gets nervous and doesn't want to stand up and do his act. This is appropriately called 'performance anxiety'.

Though usually brief, these spontaneous morning erections are an important sign that the erection mechanism is working properly and has been primed by the testosterone surge which normally occurs around wake-up time. Their loss in andropausal men is probably due to the overall decrease in free testosterone which I have found to be the key diagnostic feature and by the reduction in its daily variation with increasing age reported by other researchers.[7] This view is supported by the fact that early morning erections are one of the earliest signs of restoration of potency by testosterone and often happen within a week or two of starting treatment.

Another way in which erection problems begin is with occasional failures after a few drinks or when tired or stressed. Then they become more regular events – or non-events, depending on which way you look at it. The progress of the problem is frequently erratic and depends to some extent on the attitude of the partner. If the partner is encouraging and supportive, and willing to help by trying massage, oral sex or different positions, the problem may not progress or may even be temporary. With an uptight, dismissive and hypercritical attitude, however, performance anxiety soon sets in. After several such put downs, a man is likely to put down altogether. Nothing is more destructive of the male ego than criticism of either his ability to drive a car or to make love.

It is made even worse of course if news of his shortcomings is leaked to friends. This is why men are reluctant to own up to having this problem, even when talking to their best friend or their doctor. They try to laugh off the idea of there being any such condition as the male menopause because it is too threatening to their self-image as potent males. Yet nowadays there are a whole range of methods, including testosterone treatment in particular, which can relieve this particularly distressing symptom of the andropause.

Further problems occur because the erection starts more slowly, is more difficult to maintain and often lasts a shorter time. Sexual activity may often be rushed and is less satisfying for women, who are often slower to become aroused and to reach orgasm, especially when they themselves are post-menopausal. Anxiety makes the situation worse and can lead to premature ejaculation. This was complained of by a further quarter of my patients, as they hurried to completion while they still had an erection. Alternatively, because of the decreased sensitivity of the penis which seems to occur in low testosterone states, there may be delayed ejaculation, as was experienced by another quarter of my patients.

Another factor contributing to this problem is the lack of tone and development in the pubococcygeal (PC) muscles around the urethra and base of the bladder. These contract, as do the corresponding PC muscles around a woman's vagina, during orgasm. Like other muscles in the body, with testosterone inactivity and lack of use, their contractions get weaker and, as the patients put it, the earth no longer moves for them or their partners.

Reduced penile size, particularly when erect, sometimes accompanies severe testosterone deficiency and can also become a problem for both partners. Though it is often said that size doesn't matter, most males are acutely aware of the usual size of their penis, both flaccid and erect, and get very upset if their vital statistics are reduced.

Recent research has finally caught up with common experience when considering women's views on penile size. Though in the 1960s Masters and Johnson, the American sexologists, tried to make out that a woman's pleasure and orgasm were solely due to the little bundle of erectile tissue and nerves called the clitoris, the man who can only deliver stimulation there is likely to be operating in an erroneous rather than erogenous zone. *'Vaginal sensitivity is an anatomical reality,'* says John Perry, a clinical sexologist. While there may not always be a distinct, raised G spot, the higher part of the front wall of the vagina, especially close to the urinary passage, the urethra, is richly endowed with nerves that play a major part in helping a woman reach orgasm. Part of the secret of sexual satisfaction therefore is to have this area stimulated by the tip of the penis. This can be achieved by having the right size penis in the right size vagina or by varying the position to improve penetration.

As well as reducing the firmness of pressure on both the clitoris and G spot, testosterone inactivity can shrink the penis to the point where partners who have been physically compatible in this area throughout a long mutually enjoyable sexual relationship gradually become incompatible, to the distress of both.

Though to some extent it can be regarded as natural for the frequency and firmness of erections to reduce gradually with age, it is rapid acceleration of the process over a few months or years which should be thought of as abnormal and certainly worth investigation by the andrologist.

The causes of erectile problems are many and varied, and by the time the patient comes for treatment several overlapping factors are usually present at the same time. There may be narrowing of the arteries by which blood is pumped in to expand the penis. There may be too much blood leaking out of it through ageing veins, like a leaky cycle tyre. There may be poor nerve control, as with sugar diabetes or as a side-effect of tranquillizers, anti-depressants or the drugs used to treat high blood pressure. Also, there are certainly likely to be relationship problems, as well as the dreaded performance anxiety.

A very broad approach is therefore needed to treat what may seem like a simple mechanical fault and important though I believe such treatment is, it is not just enough to throw testosterone at the problem and hope it will go away and stay away. To do the job properly the whole man has to be screened and a range of treatments appropriate for that patient needs to be administered.

Premature Ageing

To a great extent the andropause can be thought of as a form of premature but reversible hormonal ageing. I believe that TRT offers great hope in preventing as well as treating many of the conditions associated with advancing years in the male.

Heart

Generally you're as young as your heart and brain, which largely depends on how good the circulation is to these two vital organs.

When HRT for women was first cautiously introduced over 30 years ago, doctors feared it might contribute to diseases of the blood vessels and if a menopausal woman had even a family history of heart trouble, let alone cardiac disease herself, they said HRT was not for her. Much to their surprise, actual experience has shown the reverse to be true. Women on HRT suffered half the number of heart attacks of women who didn't. So, with some reluctance, doctors have begun to change their tack and say the treatment is positively indicated in women prone to heart disease.

The situation is the same with testosterone. Over the last 50 years, most doctors, including cardiologists, have taken the view that testosterone must be bad for the heart for two totally fallacious reasons. First, under the age of 50, men get five times as many heart attacks as women in most Western countries, though the women catch up soon after that age unless they are on HRT. According to this line of reasoning, therefore, testosterone is bad for the circulation and oestrogen is good. Secondly, as already explained, because of the uniquely bad effects of the most commonly used preparation taken by mouth, methyl testosterone, and its abuse by athletes taking the wrong drugs in the wrong doses for the wrong reasons, anabolic steroids have had a very bad medical and lay press. I used to share these views myself until I met Dr Jens Møller. He led me to see testosterone as a very important and beneficial hormone for preventing and treating heart and circulatory problems. It was truly a case of seeing the light on the road to Copenhagen!

Several studies both from Britain and America have more recently shown lower levels of testosterone, and sometimes higher levels of oestrogen, in patients who later developed heart disease than in normal control subjects the same age.[8,9] Other studies have shown the benefits of testosterone and related compounds in treating a range of circulatory problems from ulcers on the feet to strokes in the brain.[10]

Circulation

Fortunately, the circulation problems experienced by the typical andropausal patient are relatively mild, and limited to cold feet and hands, especially in winter. What confuses the issue still further, however, is that the smaller blood vessels also become less stable in their reactions to heat, cold, alcohol and other stimuli. Men with this condition can experience attacks of a feeling of redness and warmth in the face, which may spread to the skin of their neck and face in warm surroundings or with alcohol.

Though less common than in menopausal women, these 'hot flushes', or 'hot flashes' as they are called in the USA, can be very marked and acutely embarrassing.[11] Imagine how a senior executive feels when he stands up to make his key presentation at a sales meeting and starts by going beetroot red, as though he is deeply ashamed of his pitch. This is made even worse by the andropausal tendency to sweat profusely, so that the man ends up looking both hot and bothered.

Though less than a quarter of the men I originally studied had hot flushes, over half complained of increased sweating, especially at night. This could sometimes be severe so that not only the night clothes but also the sheets were drenched with sweat. Some of the men felt they might have caught these symptoms off their menopausal partners!

Muscles and Bones

Another common symptom of the andropause is a general feeling of deteriorating physical condition. This is partly due to the decrease in muscle bulk and strength which accompanies the reduced level of testosterone activity. Also there are often diffuse aches, pains and stiffness both in the back and in many joints in the body, particularly the hands, ankles and knees, causing the 'Frankenstein syndrome' as the first few creaking steps are taken on rising in the morning. These are remarkably similar to the joint symptoms experienced by many menopausal women. They closely mimic arthritis, but fortunately usually show dramatic improvements with hormone treatment.

Osteoporosis, the thinning and weakening of the bones which causes older people to lose height from shrinkage and even collapse of the vertebrae, the dowager's hump in women, is also a source of much pain, unhappiness and disability in men. It is generally not as common or severe as in women and tends to come on later in life, from 70 onwards. It mainly affects the spine, where it causes back pain and stiffness, especially in the neck, and the hips, where it contributes to osteoarthritic degeneration and sometimes fractures. It has been linked with low testosterone levels in general[12] and reduced free testosterone in particular.[13]

These symptoms are made worse, and the osteoporotic process probably accelerated, by the reduced muscle size and strength which accompany the reduced activity of testosterone which occurs in the andropause.[14] Testosterone and exercise are the two main factors controlling muscle mass and strength in the male. Together with calcium and protein supply, they also have an important effect in maintaining bone mass and strength.

This is why many andropausal men complain of a general deterioration in their level of physical fitness. It is particularly noticeable if they have previously been used to high levels of athletic performance. Those who like to work out in a gym, notice that the amount of work they can perform in a session decreases, together with the number of press-ups or sit-ups. They also find their strength, in terms of the weights they can lift, goes right down. This, together with the decrease in muscle bulk that causes the pectoral muscles, biceps and thigh and buttock muscles to lose their hard-earned splendour, as well as the overall lack of drive and motivation, may even make the man give up exercise just when he most needs it.

Hair

Another area of male vanity affected by the andropause is the hair. The condition of the hair and scalp, and possibly its colour, is affected by testosterone. In the andropausal male the hair is often dull, dry and lifeless, with a tendency to dandruff. The patient may say he is going grey very quickly. Baldness in men, however, is almost entirely hereditary and if a man's hair is going to go, it will happen whatever his testosterone level, unless he has been castrated before puberty.

Though the amount of hair on the chest is also hereditary, it is affected by lifelong testosterone levels. Sometimes, if it is very much reduced and the man only has to shave once or twice a week, it can indicate a lifelong insufficiency of the hormone. But just because a man has typical male pattern baldness and plenty of hair on his chest does not mean, as is frequently assumed and quoted even by doctors who should know better, that his testosterone activity is normal.

On testosterone treatment it's interesting that some men notice a return of colour to their hair. A few have even been accused by friends and relations of using hair colour restorer. Many notice the improved condition of the hair and scalp. Also, more hair may appear on the chest, back and pubic region, which improves the man's macho image of himself.

Fortunately, testosterone treatment does not accelerate the rate of balding and may even slightly slow it down.

Skin

Like the hair, the skin is sensitive to the action of testosterone. One of the ways in which the hormone is excreted from the body is as the sebum which normally oils the skin, and makes us more water resistant and drip-dry. This is why when teenagers get a pubescent surge of testosterone, they often suffer acne from blocked pores choked with surplus sebum. This also is sometimes seen in athletes overdosing on anabolic steroids.

In the andropausal male there is insufficient sebum and so the skin, particularly on the face and hands, is noticeably dry in nearly half the cases. There may also be thinning of the skin as collagen production is decreased, which makes it look thinner and more wrinkled. Again, this process is reversed by TRT and the person often appears more 'shrink-wrapped', as one patient's wife remarked.

This wide range of mental and physical symptoms of the andropause often feels like the onset of old age and causes great alarm. The man feels he is definitely over the hill and going fast down the other side. It doesn't help if his doctor dismisses him with 'It's your age.'

Its my goal in writing this book to make the point that though age may be one of the causes of the andropause, a lot of other factors are involved, and in most cases a great deal can effectively and safely be done about it!

The first thing is to make the diagnosis and the second is to treat the condition. In my experience, the patient and his partner are often as good, if not better, than the doctor in deciding when the andropause has arrived. Many of my patients were referred to me by their wives, who had accurately assessed their symptoms, related them to their own experience of the menopause and in some desperation asked if there was any equivalent to the hormone treatment which had given them so much benefit.

Let's recap at this stage with a brief list of the symptoms of the andropause and compare them with the menopausal symptoms in women:

Symptoms of the Female Menopause

MENTAL	PHYSICAL
Fatigue	Ageing
Depression	Aches and Pains
Irritability	Sweating and Flushing
Reduced Libido	Sexual Enjoyment Decreased

Symptoms of the Male Menopause (Andropause)

MENTAL	PHYSICAL
Fatigue	Ageing
Depression	Aches and Pains

Irritability	Sweating and Flushing
Reduced Libido	Sexual Performance Decreased

The andropause is often, as you will see from the comparison above, just as obvious as the female menopause and essentially the same, but to serve as a more detailed guide I have designed the following 'Andropause Checklist', which is a shortened version of the one I use in my clinic.

This will enable you to determine with a fair degree of probability whether you or a friend or a partner are andropausal, though only assessment by a doctor experienced in this field and a full hormonal profile will confirm or exclude the diagnosis.

Andropause Checklist

	None	Slight	Medium	Severe	Extreme
1. Fatigue, tiredness or loss of energy	—	—	—	—	—
2. Depression, low or negative mood	—	—	—	—	—
3. Irritability, anger or bad temper	—	—	—	—	—
4. Anxiety or nervousness	—	—	—	—	—
5. Loss of memory or concentration	—	—	—	—	—
6. Relationship problem with partner	—	—	—	—	—
7. Loss of sex drive or libido	—	—	—	—	—
8. Erection or potency problems	—	—	—	—	—
9. Dry skin on face or hands	—	—	—	—	—
10. Excessive sweating, day or night	—	—	—	—	—
11. Backache, joint pains or stiffness	—	—	—	—	—
12. Heavy drinking, past or present	—	—	—	—	—
13. Loss of fitness	—	—	—	—	—
14. Feeling over-stressed	—	—	—	—	—

	30s	40s	50s	60s	70s+
15. The age you feel	—	—	—	—	—

TOTAL TICKS — — — — —

Multiply ticks in each
column by: 0   1   2   3   4

TOTAL SCORES — — — — —

If there has been adult mumps, orchitis or other testicular problems,
a prostate operation or inflammation, persistent urinary infection or
vasectomy, each adds four points to the total scores.

TOTAL ANDROPAUSE SCORE __

ANDROPAUSE RATING: 0–9 UNLIKELY, 10–19 POSSIBLE,
20–29 PROBABLE, 30–39 DEFINITE, 40+ ADVANCED

Chapter Three

Not the Mid-Life Crisis

Though the male mid-life crisis may precede or even overlap the male menopause or andropause, they are essentially separate and distinct conditions. In popular writing, however, they are still usually lumped together, which causes endless confusion and prevents proper consideration and understanding of either.

The word 'crisis', coming from the Greek *krisis*, meaning 'decision', suggests a time of change, transition and opportunity. It also has the meaning of a turning-point or cross-roads. It's like half-time in a football match, when the manager tells the team to change their tactics if they want to win or that they are playing just right and should keep up the good work. Hopefully you are the manager of your life, though other people may compete for the job!

Many people decide that they either have no need or no opportunity to make dramatic changes at mid-life and so the crisis may go unnoticed either by themselves or by other people. Others have agonizing decisions to make, which may take them to the brink of emotional, physical or financial disaster or even push them over the edge.

What's your mental picture of the male mid-life crisis? Like the male menopause, it's often seen as a bit of a joke. It's middle-aged men taking leave of their senses, their wives, their jobs, everything that they had worked for up to that point in their lives, and running off in search of new lives and loves.

There is even a party game simply called *MID-LIFE CRISIS* made by the Games Works, Inc. in the USA, which is really very amusing and informative on the subject. The stated objective of this board-game for '2–6 adult players in their prime' is 'to get through your middle years with more money, less stress and fewer divorce points than your opponents or to declare a MID-LIFE CRISIS, in which case you must go broke, get divorced and crack up before anyone else reaches the end of the game'. If you are in the danger zone of 35–45, or have come through this and want to look back in amusement, I recommend it to you.

One of the best and most readable of the many articles and books written on this subject was by a Dr M. W. Lear, who, as reported by Brim, in 1973 neatly summarized the dilemma of the archetypal middle-aged male:

> *The hormone production levels are dropping, the head is balding, the sexual vigour is diminishing, the stress is unending, the children are leaving, the parents are dying, the job horizons are narrowing, the friends are having their first heart attack; the past floats by in a fog of hopes not realized, opportunities not grasped, women not bedded, potentials not fulfilled, and the future is a confrontation with one's own mortality.*[1]

This last point, about looking at the hour-glass of life and seeing that so much of the limited sand of this lifetime has run through, has been recently taken up by several novelists, in particular Martin Amis in his book *The Information*.[2]

This examines the tortuous competitive interaction – it can hardly be called 'friendship' – between two middle-aged writers. Like Amis the younger, they are just turning 40, with extreme misgivings and 'comprehensive anxiety'. They are both living lies, one successfully, the other not. One has an unexpected best-selling novel on his hands and is surfing high on a wave of success, with all the attendant froth of money, public adoration and a titled wife, and is looking and feeling good for his age. The other is floundering in the foam, feeling and looking a total wash-out mentally, physically, socially and financially. He has been working on a novel called 'Untitled' for several years, which is still unpublished. 'Stacked against him in the future, he knew, were yet further novels, successively entitled "Unfinished", "Unwritten", "Unattempted" and, eventually, "Unconceived".'

What makes it worse is that in spite of all his thwarted attempts to get his book published, and the totally disastrous and humiliating response when he eventually does, this man has a lingering belief in his ability as an author, whereas he is sure the other 'can't write for toffee'.

This exploration of the seeming unfairness of life, male creativity and success and failure offers up great vistas of nothingness and cosmic and individual dissolution, or what might be termed 'Amislessness'. Unhappily, though, it fails to offer solutions to what in Amis's words is a 'terrible state, that of consciousness'.

Causes of the Mid-Life Crisis

Let's take a serious look at the causes of what I believe is a genuine and sometimes profound emotional crisis in a man's life, and how it differs from the male menopause or andropause.

Many of the patients with the classic picture of the andropause give an equally characteristic story of a series of events precipitating a mid-life crisis some five to ten years earlier. It is important to differentiate between the two conditions because the confusion between the two means that they are often bracketed together and laughed off as a temporary emotional crisis without any physical cause. They are then considered to be just an excuse for men to behave badly toward the women in their lives, and avoid their social or family responsibilities.

While the male menopause is mainly a hormonal condition due to insufficient testosterone activity, as described earlier, it can also have profound emotional effects. The male mid-life crisis is essentially emotional in origin but if severe enough or long enough may have physical consequences, especially if alcohol or drugs are used to blunt the pain of the crisis.

Typically, the age group most prone to the male mid-life crisis is around 40, mainly between 35 and 45. This is earlier than, but may occasionally overlap, the andropause, which usually starts around the age of 50, say 45 to 55, though it can sometimes be earlier or later.

Many, if not most, mid-life crises go unnoticed and are passed off as the effects of a change of job, a change of house or a change of spouse. Only occasionally does the crisis turn into a drama, as can be seen daily in the lives and biographies of public figures, showbusiness personalities and politicians.[3,4,5,6,7]

What makes a man prone to a full-scale mid-life crisis? Well, anything that destabilizes him from childhood onwards. This can include being born with a sensitive or artistic nature, distant or unloving parents, the loss of one parent, particularly the father, at an early age, loss or separation from a loved one or role model and repeated failure or, paradoxically, repeated success in his career.[8] As Oscar Wilde said, 'In this life there are only two tragedies. One is not getting what one wants, and the other is getting it.'

There may be an existential crisis in which the man may feel he is stuck in a career which either under-extends or over-extends him so that he is faced with rust-out or burn-out. He may also be in a dead-end job or in a marriage that has gone stale and having to choose between staying in that relationship or facing the traumas of divorce, particularly the pain of separation from his children, and often having to start over again financially. These perils of the 'roaring forties' of his life may lead on to the '3-D syndrome' of depression, drink and divorce which, as we shall see, can set the scene for the andropause to follow.

Differences between the Mid-Life Crisis and the Andropause

Let's run through a checklist to spell out the differences:
Age – The mid-life crisis usually is confined to the ages of 35 to 45, while the andropause is characteristically 45 to 55, as with the female menopause. However, if there was previous damage to the testes, such as from mumps, alcohol or vasectomy, the andropause may arrive earlier.
Childhood – A disturbed, unsupportive childhood, one starved of love and affection, especially if accompanied by physical or mental abuse, is much more common

in the background of someone experiencing the mid-life crisis.

Triggers – The death or serious illness of a parent or close friend is a common trigger of the mid-life crisis, as such events bring you face to face with your own mortality. They make you feel that you are next in the firing-line, which in turn brings up thoughts and feelings about the meaning of your life and your past, present and future goals and achievements.[9]

Paradoxically, this crisis can come after a period of success even more often than after a dismal failure. It may even come when you find the love of your life, either in a person or an occupation, but feel it is too late or an impossible dream. As 'crisis' suggests, it is decision time, but you agonize over the choices. You consider changing your job, your partner or your whole way of life. By contrast, the andropause comes after redundancy, after heavy financial losses, after the business has failed or after divorce, rather than during the period leading up to them.

Relationships – The crisis is by its nature often very much about personal and business relationships. Questions about whether you want to go living with that person. or working with another, or in that organization, are often uppermost in your mind. You think about them again and again, and you even may dream about them again and again at night.

During the andropause, you are more likely to feel too weary to want to make any changes and too tired to even dream about doing so. Because of this lethargy, your marriage and business relationships may be falling to pieces around you, but you feel powerless to do anything about it.

Sex drive – This is most often increased during the crisis, either as a form of escapism, or as a conscious or subconscious way of bringing matters to a head. Sometimes, however, when a man is depressed by these events, as with other forms of depression, the libido may decrease. With the andropause the libido is almost always decreased, though occasionally there may be an affair to try to revive waning sexual powers.

Potency – As with most things there are few absolute rules about this, but apart from obvious physical causes such as diabetes, or the side-effects of medicines such as those used to lower blood pressure or treat depression, or where triggered by severe psycho-sexual problems, only during the andropause is potency consistently decreased over several months or years.

Physical symptoms – Fatigue, aches, pains and stiffness in the joints, night sweats and other physical symptoms which are typical of the andropause are usually absent in the crisis.

Hormone patterns – These are nearly always normal during the crisis, unless there is deep depression or heavy drinking. Though total testosterone is often normal during the andropause, the free, biologically active testosterone is typically decreased, as described in the next chapter. There are also often other more subtle markers of this condition to confirm the diagnosis which can be found by careful and extensive hormone profiles of the blood.

Responses to treatment – Treatment of the crisis is mainly by counselling and support to help the person resolve the issues which are troubling them. Tranquillizers or anti-depressants can occasionally be effective for short-term treatment if anxiety or depression is overwhelming. However they can be addictive and actually delay solving the problems which life has thrown up.

Testosterone will not help the person experiencing the crisis but is likely to bring dramatic benefit to those suffering the miseries of the andropause.

Mid-Life Crisis Checklist

1. Age	*30s*	*40s*	*50s*	*60s*
2. Death of Parent within	*1 yr*	*2 yrs*	*3 yrs*	*4 yrs*
3. Death of Close Friend within	*1 yr*	*2 yrs*	*3 yrs*	*4 yrs*
4. Change or Loss of Job within	*1 yr*	*2 yrs*	*3 yrs*	*4 yrs*
5. Change or Loss of Partner within	*1 yr*	*2 yrs*	*3 yrs*	*4 yrs*
6. Satisfaction with Present Partner	*Bad*	*Poor*	*Fair*	*Good*
7. Satisfaction with Present Work	*Bad*	*Poor*	*Fair*	*Good*
8. Satisfaction with your Childhood	*Bad*	*Poor*	*Fair*	*Good*
9. Confidence about Role in Life	*Bad*	*Poor*	*Fair*	*Good*
10. Sex Drive (Libido)	*Excess*	*Average*	*Fair*	*Bad*
11. Potency (Erections)	*Excess*	*Average*	*Fair*	*Bad*
12. Mental Energy	*Excess*	*Average*	*Fair*	*Bad*
13. Physical Energy	*Excess*	*Average*	*Fair*	*Bad*
14. Creativity	*Excess*	*Average*	*Fair*	*Bad*
15. Day Dreaming	*Regular*	*Often*	*Seldom*	*None*
16. Night Dreaming	*Regular*	*Often*	*Seldom*	*None*
17. Heavy Drinking	*Regular*	*Often*	*Seldom*	*None*
18. Tranquillizer Use	*Regular*	*Often*	*Seldom*	*None*
19. Thoughts about Dying	*Regular*	*Often*	*Seldom*	*None*
20. Thoughts about Major Life Changes	*Regular*	*Often*	*Seldom*	*None*

TOTAL TICKS

Multiply ticks in each column by:	3	2	1	0

TOTAL SCORES
TOTAL MID-LIFE CRISIS SCORE

MID-LIFE CRISIS RATING: 0–9 UNLIKELY, 10–19 POSSIBLE, 20–29 PROBABLE, 30–39 DEFINITE, 40+ ADVANCED

The Game of Mid-Life Crisis Survival

There is a James Bond story called *You Only Live Twice*: For some men a second life really does begin at 40. For many, either on a plateau or steadily on the way up, this period may just be a natural continuation of the old life and they don't experience it as a crisis. For others there is a period of great unrest and inner turbulence, the 'Dark Night of the Soul', but they come through and either decide to climb on up to fresh peaks or settle for comfortable life in the valley. A few, unfortunately, fall down one of the slippery slopes of addiction to alcohol or drugs, sexual over-activity or risk-taking behaviour and may or may not survive the experience. Others get lost and spend the rest of their lives wandering aimlessly or fall prey to the black bear of depression. Sometimes they find themselves and make successful changes in their lives, or sometimes the climate of opinion or fashion changes in their favour and they get a helicopter ride up the mountain.

Often this crisis is very publicly seen in showbusiness celebrities whose careers have taken off or whose unstable relationships have broken down. These events bring with them large-scale publicity which can lead to what has recently been described by the British journalist A. A. Gill as 'over-exposure on the media mountain'. Blinded by flashbulbs, exhausted by interviews which deplete them of their vital stores of essential nutrients such as sensible things to say, and constantly breathing the narcotic oxygen of publicity, they succumb to 'media mountain madness'. In the terminal stages of this, fortunately usually only seen high up on the Hallucinatory Hills of Hollywood, but with an increasing number of cases now appearing around New York, they stumble around, pursued by packs of ravening reporters, until they fall into bottomless chasms of obscurity or are buried under an avalanche of hype. Some never recover. Like the British comedian Tony Hancock, they may commit suicide, or, like Peter Sellers, drive themselves to heart attacks, which are often due to the inner enemies of anger and despair.

Surviving the Mid-Life Crisis

There is a great deal to learn from all these stories about how to come through your own mid-life crisis, if you are having one, or how to help other people through theirs. If you can see clearly how you yourself or others got lost on the mountain you may be able to get down, or help guide others down, or you may decide to call in a professional mid-life mountain rescue team.

Make a Map

For the person who decides that they have reached mid-life, or those trying to help them, it helps to make a map. Where are you now and where, if anywhere, do you want to get to? Some people are destined to climb one peak of achievement or creativity, often in their twenties or thirties, and then plateau off at mid-life or go downhill. Others achieve a second, perhaps even higher peak later in life, having successfully dealt with their mid-life crisis using the experience, knowledge and wisdom built up in the first half of their lives. This can happen in all walks of life, but particularly with writers, who breathe in experience and breathe out prose, with applied scientists, and sometimes with businessmen, who may hit the financial rocks in mid-life, but learn important lessons and go on to rebuild their empires.

Decisions again. What realistically are your goals and

how worthwhile are they to you? How high do you want to climb? How much effort are you willing to put in and what risks are you willing to take? Are you content with what you have achieved and got out of life so far? As the financier Bernie Cornfeld, who created the huge financial bubble of Investors in Overseas Securities, IOS, or, as it could have been more accurately called, IOU, put it, 'Do you sincerely want to be rich?' Do you? Or do you have other priorities?

Resources for the Journey

Having decided where you want to go, or at least the direction, you need to make a full and fearless inventory of your resources in terms of health, finances and abilities. Don't forget to include the emotional support of your family and friends among your assets, as they can be crucial, especially if you are making radical changes to your life.

Also make a list of your weaknesses and the emotional baggage you are carrying. How much of it is necessary and how much can you leave behind you? How much 'unfinished business' do you have with a difficult childhood or family relationships? Could you finish it, if necessary with the help of a psychotherapist or analyst? What are your addictions, if any: alcohol, drugs, work, chocolate, food, sex? Think about where you can get help with these, because they can cripple you on the next part of your journey or even stop you ever getting started. What's your Achilles heel and how you can guard it?

In the final analysis you have to decide what you can change in yourself, as it has to be accepted that you can't change the world or others. If you decide you do wish, and are able, to make changes, probably the best idea is to follow the business tradition of making a five year plan to aid you in your journey and decide what you would like to have achieved by then. 'Realistic, but optimistic' is probably the best motto, but think carefully whether you will be able to live at peace with yourself and those around you if you realize your new ambition or continue with your old one.

If you think you can cope with or have coped with the hazards of the mid-life crisis, you may well be interested in lessening your chances of experiencing the andropause. The next chapter tells you how it happens and how your response to the mid-life crisis may have either set you up for it or protected you from ever getting it.

Chapter Four

How It Happens

Why should one man suffer all the miseries of the male menopause in his forties or fifties and another in his seventies or eighties escape them entirely? I am reminded of the Viking warrior, cold, damp and miserable on a bleak landscape in a thunderstorm, shaking his fist at the sky and crying out, 'Why me, O Lord? Why me?' After a pause for thought, a thunderous voice from the heavens replies, 'Why not?'

Similarly, though the roots of this condition can usually be traced to one or several of the hammer blows of fate which affect us throughout life, sometimes its causes remain unknown.

Let's look first at how testosterone is produced and its key role as a major contributor to the force of destiny which shapes our lives, 'rough-hew them as we may'.

Hormone of Kings – King of Hormones

The hormone testosterone brings us into being. It regulates the sex drive in both men and women, it develops the male sexual characteristics such as dominance, drive, assertiveness, strength, body shape, hairiness and even odour in the form of pheromones. It governs sperm production as well as potency and therefore has the casting vote on whether or not conception takes place.

It is a major factor in deciding, both physically and mentally, whether we develop into a man or a woman, a homosexual or heterosexual, a poet or a boxer, a wimp or a champ. As described in the book by Anne Moir and David Jesell, *Brain Sex: The real difference between men and women*,[1] it even literally shapes our brain, decides our creativity, intellectual skills, thought patterns, and our drive and determination to explore ideas and follow them through. It is an overriding influence in controlling not only our potential, but also the use we make of it. It governs our sexual and social history.

Testosterone also affects our health throughout life – how we grow as children, whether we thrive, whether we become a muscular Adonis in our teens or a weed with acne, even whether we are likely to die in a fight or motorcycle accident in our youth. It affects to what extent stress will undermine our health in middle age and how we will die from the premature ageing that its deficiency can cause, especially in the heart. Therefore it controls both our vitality and longevity.

As already mentioned, it can also be regarded as the 'success hormone'. A study funded by the National Institute of Health in the United States compared testosterone levels with personality type in over 1,700 men. It was found, according to Dr John McKinley, the medical statistician who analysed the results, that typically the male with high testosterone, the High-T Guy, *'attempts to influence and control other people ... expresses his opinion forcibly and his anger freely, and ... dominates social interactions'*. Having innately and persistently high levels of testosterone seems to make these men hard-driving, competitive and sometimes more successful.[2]

However, once these patterns of behaviour are established, though lowering testosterone activity may cause them to fade, treatment with even high doses of the hormone will only restore them to normal for that individual and not overshoot to cause aggression, anti-social activities or hyper-sexuality.

These findings closely mirrored those of Professor James Dabbs, a psychologist at Georgia State University. He studied 5,000 Vietnam War veterans and found that anti-social 'sensation seeking' behaviour more often occurred in high-testosterone men with little education and low income jobs. Those with more education and money had opportunities for a wider range of outlets for this type of behaviour. 'They can do things that are both exciting and sociably acceptable – driving fast cars rather than stealing them, and arguing instead of fighting,' said Dabbs. He also found that both men and women in more extrovert and expressive occupations such as actors, entertainers, football players and even women lawyers had high levels of testosterone, while clergymen had low levels. In this way it seems that testosterone affects every aspect of our lives as men.[3]

Testosterone Production

The command centre for testosterone control is the brain. This has a variety of interrelated checks and balances which promote or suppress production, according to the needs of the body at that stage in life and at that particular time.

The highest functional part of the brain, the cerebral

cortex, stimulates testosterone production when we are aroused and feel we are succeeding in life. When we are bored or angry with our partners or overstressed and feel we are losing in life's battles, our testosterone goes down. These reactions are controlled day to day by the hypothalamus, the 'impresario', at the base of the brain, and hour to hour by the pituitary gland, the 'conductor of the hormone orchestra of the body'. This vital gland is the size and shape of a small cherry in the adult and is suspended by a short stalk from the hypothalamus, from which it receives its regulatory messages. Accordingly it produces a wide variety of key hormones which stimulate or suppress the various glands in the body, including the testes.

The pituitary hormones which control the sexual organs in both men and women are called gonadotrophins. There are two of these, named according to their functions in the female. One is called follicle stimulating hormone (FSH), because in the female it stimulates the growth of the follicles in the ovary which contain the eggs, though in the male it is mainly concerned with promoting sperm production. The other is called luteinizing hormone (LH), and regulates the production of oestrogen by the ovaries in the female and testosterone by the testes in the male. However recent research suggests that there are some interactions between these hormones in controlling testosterone production.[4]

Research has shown that over 95 per cent of the 6–7 mg of the testosterone produced daily by the young male comes from the 500 million 'interstitial' or 'Leydig' cells in the testes, the remaining 5 per cent coming from the adrenal glands capping both kidneys. Blood testosterone levels in men are usually 10 to 20 times those in women, where the adrenals and ovaries are the main production sites. Eunuchs are therefore likely to have the same testosterone levels as women, just as men usually have the same oestrogen levels as post-menopausal women whose ovaries have stopped its production.

The raw material from which testosterone is synthesized in the body is cholesterol, and it was shown in 1984 by a group of Finnish researchers that low fat diets, especially when the proportion of the 'healthy' unsaturated fats was increased, lowered both total and free testosterone levels in the blood. This may be one explanation for the sad fact that any decrease in heart disease produced by these diets or cholesterol lowering drugs tends to be outweighed by increasing deaths from suicide, homicide and accidents, some of which might be linked to the testosterone deficient andropausal mood changes.[5]

It seems unfair that the limp-lettuce diet foisted on an unsuspecting public by dietary dogmatists might be contributing to lower testosterone activity and the apparently increasing level of erection problems in men. One wonders what the more drastic cholesterol lowering drugs that some of my patients were put on just before the onset of andropausal symptoms are doing to their androgen levels.

On the other hand we have the sexual athletic performances of the sixteenth-century legendary lover Giacomo Casanova, who boosted his testosterone levels with large numbers of raw eggs before each of his amorous marathons. It was reputedly the pox rather than heart disease which killed him at the age of 73.

Also, as pointed out in my book *The Western Way of Death: Stress, tension and heart disease*,[6] 75 per cent of the cholesterol circulating in the bloodstream is made in the body by the liver, and is increased by stress, and only 25 per cent comes in from the diet. Stress has other harmful effects, such as raising blood pressure and increasing blood clotting, so there is a lot of evidence that where heart disease is concerned *'It's not so much a matter of what you eat as what's eating you.'*

One of the many compounds produced on the long production line leading from cholesterol to testosterone rejoices in the name of dehydroepiandrosterone, known to its aficionados as DHEA. This is an interesting steroid because its production rate is directly related to that of testosterone and it has been shown to decrease linearly with age, which gives further evidence about the possible origin of the andropause. It has even been given clinically in one trial on ageing men by Dr Etienne-Emil Baulieu at the Institute of Health and Medical Research in Paris and provided some of the benefits of testosterone treatment. However it is more expensive than the latter and seems a roundabout way of promoting its synthesis, if that is what is needed. Also, some may be converted into oestrogen, which antagonizes testosterone actions and so in certain patients it could be counterproductive. However it is certainly worth looking at further as a way of increasing natural testosterone production in the body.

Similarly a hormone from the pituitary gland, growth hormone, can boost the action of testosterone and has been claimed to have rejuvenated a small number of American veterans on whom it was tried.[7] However it needed twice weekly injections, was about 10 times as expensive as testosterone and unlike that very safe medication, caused rises in blood pressure and sugar levels.

Testosterone throughout Life

Even in the womb, there are larger amounts of testosterone present in the blood of males than females. This starts as early as six weeks after conception, reaches a peak of five to six times higher at 23 weeks and then falls back to female levels at about six months of intra-uterine life. By that time, of course, development of all the organs in the body are nearly complete, and mentally and physically the male or female die is cast.

The development of the penis and the descent of the testes into the scrotum prepared to receive them are largely under the control of testosterone, and it also affects the brain, where the balance in function between the two hemispheres is supposed to be influenced by this hormonal difference. The mountain of inescapable evidence that men are different from women in a whole range of aptitudes, skills and abilities, and that these differences depend much more on hormonal nature than social nurture, is brilliantly reviewed in *Brain Sex*.

After birth there is another surge of testosterone in the male, going up almost to adult male levels. It starts at about two weeks, reaches a peak at 10 weeks and then drops back to female levels at six months and stays there till puberty. These early months are also a period of active brain growth and development during which further sexual differentiation can arise. It seems likely that the traumas of birth and the first six months of life, such as prematurity, failure of maternal bonding, malnutrition and infections, might all reduce testosterone production and be factors which predispose a sickly infant to be a sickly adult.

At puberty in the male, the testosterone rises rapidly, reaching a maximum of about 20 to 30 times the infant level at about age 18. This causes the pubertal development of hair on the face, armpits, pubes and, to a more variable extent which is mainly due to hereditary factors, on the rest of the body, particularly arms, legs and chest. Whether a man goes bald or not later in life again seems to be more down to heredity than hormones, unless he is castrated before puberty. It's what's in his genes that decides whether he keeps his hair for life, rather than what's in his jeans.

Also at puberty, the testes enlarge and descend into the scrotum, libido surges, the penis enlarges, erections occur spontaneously, particularly at night and in the early morning, and if not relieved by masturbation or intercourse, spontaneous emissions or 'wet dreams' happen, all of which can be associated with an unreasonable amount of adolescent emotional upset and guilt. At the same time the voice tone deepens and 'breaks', due to thickening of the vocal cords, and the excess hormones and the pheromones are poured out in the sweat and skin oil, the sebum, which causes the social and physical discomforts of acne. Helped by growth hormone from the pituitary gland, there is an increase in muscle and bone growth in the male, but above a certain level testosterone switches off the latter, and between the ages of 18 and 20 growth usually ceases.

In eunuchs, and men with low levels of testosterone because the testes fail to develop or descend, growth may continue and the man gets taller than other men in his family. At the other extreme, high levels of testosterone may arrest bone growth, and a highly sexed and hairy, shorter man result. This could be the hormonal history of cuddly Dudley Moore, once described as a 'sex-thimble', and the far less cuddly but also sexually active Napoleon Bonaparte. The statue of him (Napoleon, that is, not Dudley) standing naked in heroic pose on show in Apsley House at Hyde Park Corner in London indicates that he was well endowed in sexual structure as well as function. However, by the time he died, a beaten man possibly suffering lead poisoning,

Napoleon was found to have severe genital atrophy. Wonderful are the permutations and combinations of heredity, hormones and history which produce the individual physique and temperament.

Testosterone and the Male Menopause

One of the main reasons why the idea of the male menopause has proved so controversial is that unlike the female menopause, where there is a clear and easily measurable precipitous drop in oestrogen level, it is difficult to show any such fall in the male suffering similar symptoms. To understand why this is so, we must enterprisingly 'boldly go' a little deeper into the mechanics of testosterone control and action.

The small but vital amounts of testosterone produced in the testes are immediately swept away round the body in the bloodstream and are mainly bound to a special carrier protein called sex hormone binding globulin. This SHBG, as it is usually called, is a key player in this 'Who stole the testosterone?' mystery, since it grabs the hormone and runs, and seems reluctant to part with it. The more SHBG there is, the less free, active, 'bioavailable' testosterone is able to get out of the blood into the cells to do its job.

The availability of the testosterone can be measured as the 'free androgen index', or FAI, which is the total testosterone level in the blood divided by the SHBG level multiplied by 100, and is usually between 70 and 100 per cent. It is when the FAI falls below 50 per cent that symptoms of the andropause usually appear. This has been one of the key findings in my research.

The way in which the body regulates the amount of testosterone available at any one time works well in youth, when there is usually plenty of testosterone and its level of activity is controlled by a roughly equivalent amount of SHBG. If testosterone levels drop temporarily for any reason, the SHBG falls to compensate for this, and so the amount of testosterone available, expressed by the FAI, is kept constant. However, later in life, especially around the age of 50, this 'testostat' mechanism often seems to break down and the andropause results. A car-dealer patient of mine called SHBG 'Sex Hand-Brake Globulin' because he felt his hormonal engine was revving, but his brakes were on.

What goes wrong in this key part of the body's hormonal balance? There are two possible explanations. The first is that the amount of testosterone 'income' falls due to understimulation of the testes by the hypothalamus and pituitary, deficiency of raw materials for its production and wearing out of the testes. The second is that the 'expenditure' rises, in terms of amount of testosterone taken up by the SHBG and that used up in repairing the ravages of age, stress, alcohol and other forms of wear and tear. Also, the cells all over the body which are the targets for Cupid's testosterone arrows may become tougher with age, more difficult to penetrate and less responsive to its effects.

A life-long programme of research by a Belgian professor, Alex Vermeulen at the University of Ghent, has shown that all stages in the production and action of testosterone can be affected by the ageing process.[8] Particularly after middle age, the amount of testosterone produced falls because of ageing of the interstitial cells that produce it in the testis. In the 1960s, this was made very clear because the amount of testosterone appearing in the urine was found to drop steadily with age, since it represents the 'free', active hormone.[9] Other doctors have shown that from about the age of 40 onwards, testicular size and the amount of free testosterone began to decrease, and the pituitary driving force increased to try and compensate.[10]

However, what still confuses critics of the male menopause theory even to the present day is that the level of total testosterone as measured in the blood only falls slightly up to the age of 70. This is because the hormone is being held in the blood by rising levels of SHBG and so less is 'bio-available' to be taken up by the target receptors in the tissues or excreted in the urine.[11,12] This has been confirmed in the first 400 of my male menopause patients, where only 13 per cent showed abnormally low total testosterone levels in the blood, but, mainly because of raised SHBG levels, about 75 per cent had a low free androgen index. About 70 per cent also showed raised levels of the pituitary gonadotrophin hormones which stimulate the testis, the LH and FSH, which confirms that the level of testosterone activity is insufficient for the body's needs.

As already mentioned, this situation was recognized and proved from urinary studies in the 1940s, but thanks to the complications introduced by blood tests, doctors are still able to argue about it to this day. Many patients have come to me saying that they had classic andropausal symptoms, but their doctors measured their total testosterone level, found it normal or low normal, and said that there was nothing wrong with their hormones and it must all be psychological. Fortunately some patients persevere in the belief that it is their hormones that are out of order rather than their minds, get the additional tests done to complete the diagnosis and start rationally based testosterone treatment.

Early Disturbances

The normal patterns in hormonal development can be delayed, arrested or modified at any stage of life. About 10 per cent of the male menopause patients I have seen probably had lower than normal testosterone levels from puberty onwards. These cases were sometimes due to the testes never having functioned properly because of failure to descend into the scrotum, only partially descending, or retracting back into the abdomen too easily.

These varying degrees of partial non-functioning or impaired development of the testis may not be obvious, or indeed interfere with sexual characteristics or function noticeably till middle-age or later.

The Oestrogen Threat to the Male

As well as the decreasing amounts and activity of testosterone, the threat to male fertility and virility can be explained by increasing exposure to xeno-oestrogens, chemicals in the environment with actions similar to those of the female hormone oestrogen, and to anti-androgens, which have recently been found to have an anti-testosterone action.[13,14]

Oestrogens, though essential for the development of female characteristics, seem to work against the actions of testosterone in the male. Derived from everything from plastics to pesticides, they are thought to be having a harmful effect on fertility and the sexual development of male offspring, and to be even contributing to rising testicular and prostate cancer rates. Their effect was seen most dramatically in women given the strong synthetic oestrogen stilboestrol during pregnancy to reduce the chances of a miscarriage. When their sons were born, a considerable number had undescended testes and abnormal genital development. Later in life they were also found to be infertile because of low sperm counts.

For a wide and increasing variety of reasons men seem to be drowning in a sea of oestrogens. Even the uterine bath water they swim in during the first nine months of life is laced with rising levels of such hormonally-active compounds. Evidence of this is the increasing numbers of boys being born with hormonally caused birth defects in their sexual characteristics. This is especially marked in the condition known as hypospadias, where the penis is poorly developed and opens towards the base rather than at the tip. Also, because of the continuing influence of these oestrogenic compounds, the testes increasingly often fail to descend from the abdomen into the scrotum, which not only decreases their ability to produce sperm, but also reduces their testosterone producing capacity.[15]

Perhaps future generations of archaeologists will come across thick strata of plastic bags, marking the demise of *homo plasticus* or 'plastic bag man' who was neutered by the by-products of the consumer society.

Exposure to oestrogens at any time of life can have a bad effect in the male, but particularly around the time of puberty. One patient of mine, when at university in his late teens, made the mistake of telling his college doctor that he felt over-sexed. The doctor over-reacted by giving him a month's course of oestrogen. It worked well – his libido died overnight and he was able to concentrate on his studies. The unfortunate thing was that his libido never recovered, he never married or had children, and when he came to see me at the age of 45 it seemed that he had a premature andropause, with no other apparent cause.

An interesting sub-group of my patients which

appeared to show occupational risk factors for the andropause were farmers. The health of these 'front-line' troops in the agrochemical arms race towards greater productivity and profitability makes an interesting study in relation to chemical pollution of the environment.[16]

In some the causative agent of their symptoms appeared obvious. The main relevant feature of their case histories was that they had worked on farms when they were young men caponizing chickens or turkeys with oestrogen pellet implants or creams to make the birds plumper and more tender. Unfortunately, though it might be considered poetic justice, they must themselves have taken in large amounts of oestrogen, either by absorption through the skin or lungs, or by eating the birds shortly after the treatment, which caused them to partly become caponized themselves.

In a similar case concerning cattle, an andropausal patient from Canada recently told me how on his farm he and his brother often ate beef without waiting for the 48-hour so-called safety limit to expire, after giving their cattle long-acting hormone cocktails supposed to promote growth for up to three months. Either they misread the instructions or they were being seriously misled by the manufacturers of these dollar-a-shot mixtures.

Clinically, as well as severe andropausal symptoms of fatigue, depression, irritability and loss of libido and potency, these farm-workers often showed enlargement of their breasts (gynaecomastia), testicular atrophy, low total testosterone, high SHBG giving a reduced free androgen index, and elevated FSH and LH levels.

Another sub-group of farmers, however, had similar symptoms, but gave a history of exposure to other potentially anti-testosterone hormones or pesticides used in farming. Here the clinical and endocrine features were less marked. Fortunately both groups responded well to androgen treatment, either orally or by testosterone pellet implant.

The latter group, however, could well have been examples of anti-androgen activity from any one of a wide range of anti-microbial agents, pesticides and fungicides. For example, it was observed in 1971 that coccidiostats given to chickens produced maximum weight gain for minimum food intake, but they were banned because they caused men to develop large womanly breasts and infertility.

A wide range of drugs used in medicine are known to have this property. Detailed studies of such compounds, taking into account the possibly differing effects of different forms of the same molecule (stereoisomers), may give clues as to their complex hormonal interactions.

My first Professor of Biochemistry at the Middlesex Hospital in London, Sir Charles Dodds, working with a group in Oxford, was the first to describe xenooestrogens in an article in *Nature* dated 5 February 1938: 'The Oestrogenic Activity of Certain Synthetic Compounds'. He compared the structure of what he proposed should be called 'stilboestrol', which his group had just synthesized, with the naturally occurring hormone called oestrone.[17]

Later the same year he described the oestrogenic actions of a range of related compounds and noted the 'large effects of relatively small changes' in related molecules.[18] These two historic papers set the scene for mass production of oestrogenic compounds for both therapeutic and veterinary purposes, and could explain some of our present concerns on the effects of xenooestrogens and androgen receptor antagonists.

Just as small changes in molecules can greatly increase their oestrogenic activity, so apparently minor modifications can make them much more powerful anti-androgens. This was dramatically demonstrated by Kelce and his co-workers in an article in *Nature* in June 1995 which showed how the major and persistent metabolite of DDT, *p,p'*-DDE, had little oestrogenic activity, but 15 times the anti-androgen effect of the parent compound.[19]

This was one-fifth of the potency, if that is the right word, of the most powerful anti-androgen used in medical and veterinary practice, flutamide, the well-known side-effects of which are severe andropausal symptoms and gynaecomastia. The similarities in the structural formulae of these compounds, together with that of the known anti-androgen vinclozolin, used in agriculture as a fungicide, are apparent when you look at their molecular structures.

Fortunately, the chemical castration of man and beast by the use of overtly oestrogenic compounds in veterinary practice was banned in the UK in 1986 and in the remainder of the European Union by a hormonal growth promoter ban in 1988. However the practice still continues as an underground activity in some countries, along with the dangerous business of giving a large range of chemical cocktails to many different farmyard animals to improve the amount and texture of meat, or more recently milk yield by using genetically engineered bovine somatotrophin (rBST).

As well as recognized hormonally active products, it is suggested that the effects on both oestrogen and androgen receptors of a wide range of products used in veterinary medicine and agriculture should be investigated as a matter of urgency, and any of the heavy commercial pressures to reverse the EU ban on hormonal growth promoters resisted until a great deal more research has been done to clear such compounds of any possible threat to human health. It is alarming to note that in Belgium food inspectors trying to obtain meat samples to stem this tide of agricultural abuse of hormones have been threatened and even allegedly murdered. As in athletics, more random and widespread checks, leading to legal action where necessary, together with a public information campaign emphasizing the medical dangers to producers and consumers alike, should be brought in. This in the long term could be a greater health threat than 'mad cow disease' (BSE).

It took 50 years to learn the lesson spelt out by Sir Charles Dodds in 1938 and ban oestrogenic substances from veterinary practice, but now apparently we have a seven year itch to unlearn it. Should we perhaps be going 'back to nature' to learn the 1995 message from Kelce and his co-workers about the possible anti-androgenic effects of a wide range of agrochemicals?

Viral and Bacterial Infections

Infections can also be linked to testicular and other damage. Two thousand years ago Hippocrates recognized mumps sometimes caused shrinkage and infertility later in life. In general, anything which affects fertility in the male is also likely to influence testosterone production. However, it is not appreciated even by the medical profession how a long-forgotten childhood illness can contribute to precipitating the andropause 30 or 40 years later.

The testis seems only liable to be damaged by the mumps virus, and perhaps other viruses, from the first stirrings of puberty onwards. This seems to be because this is a time of intense activity, cell division and growth in the testis.

Before the age of 10 or 12, mumps is a highly infectious viral illness passing from child to child, causing a mild fever and the very characteristic swelling of the parotid salivary glands in front of both ears, which usually passes off without complications within a few days. An attack of mumps at this age is usually entirely harmless and gives valuable immunity which frequently lasts for life.

If he picks up the infection any time beyond this age, however, a man is likely to be generally more ill and one or both testes may become very painful, swollen and inflamed, a condition known as orchitis. This very uncomfortable condition, sometimes described by song title 'Great Balls of Fire', can last one or two weeks or even longer. It then subsides, often leaving scarring of one or both testes, which may be shown by shrinkage or softening.[20]

Infertility after mumps is fortunately uncommon, but there may be in many cases damage to the testosterone producing cells which becomes apparent later in life. Eleven per cent of my andropause patients gave a history of mumps after the age of 12 and in these cases, which tended to be the younger patients, there was often no other obvious cause. These are good reasons why more immunization of boys should be carried out early in infancy.

Though mumps is by far the most obvious and common virus attacking the testis, there is some evidence that a wide range of others may sometimes be involved, and their influence overlooked because the orchitis is a less prominent feature of a generalized feverish illness making the patient feel rotten all over. Again, it is probably when the testis is most active, around the age of puberty, that it is most susceptible to damage by viruses.

Another virus which has been definitely recorded as occasionally causing orchitis is glandular fever, also known as infectious mononucleosis or the 'kissing disease', as outbreaks seemed to spread among boys and girls in this way, though this could just be parental propaganda.[21]

Sometimes patients date their andropausal symptoms from some unidentified viral illness, though whether this directly affected their testosterone production or was just the last straw that caused a hormonal breakdown is unclear. The fatigue, depression and loss of libido that accompanies many viral conditions, especially myalgic encephalitis (ME), can mimic many of the symptoms of the male menopause, and careful history taking and hormonal tests are needed to distinguish between them. Similarly, the general malaise affecting patients during a severe attack of jaundice, whether due to hepatitis A, B or the newly discovered insidious variety C, is likely to reduce the patients' testosterone production, whether the testes are directly affected or not.

Other infections of the testes and prostate also seem liable to affect testosterone levels. Both so-called 'nonspecific urethritis', a common cause of penile soreness and discharge, and the better known sexually transmitted diseases such as syphilis or gonorrhoea can bring about a reduction in testosterone. Sometimes infections of the prostate and testis can also occur after surgery to the prostate or bladder, with the same result.

The possible involvement of so many infections in contributing to the male menopause underlines the need for doctors involved in its treatment to take a full case history. Much further research is needed to see which infections, at what age, need to be avoided or treated to maintain full testicular function.

Stress

Lack of desire and performance in relation to sex are commonly seen in men under stress, particularly when they grow older. While younger men, especially those going through the male mid-life crisis, may use sex as a means of relieving tension or trying to restore confidence, over the age of 50 the stressed male is more likely to go right off it. This is a natural biological reaction and is seen throughout the animal kingdom.

Stress assessed as excessive 'life events' appeared to be the factor which precipitated the andropause in over half of the men seen in my clinic. This was much more evident with the stresses of failure and defeat in life's battles than those of success. Divorce, insolvency, heavy financial losses, unemployment, recession in business and losing court cases were all big put downs, mentally and then physically. Conversely, successful remarriage, the start of a new relationship, getting a desired job or promotion or winning the lottery could fan the flames, or sometimes even the ashes, of both virility and vitality. Even a good relaxing holiday can sometimes have the same effect, though all too often the benefits fade as rapidly as a sun tan when the man returns to his stressful workaday world.

Why does stress have such a powerful effect on people's sex lives? Obviously it is partly a direct psychological effect. If the brain, which has been described as the biggest sex organ in the body, is directing its attentions mainly towards survival in the urban jungle, sexual activity will have a low priority.

Anxiety, too, is a definite turn-off, and performance anxiety, as we have seen, can be a self-fulfilling prophesy.

Excessive stress – 'stress overload' – can also act by

reducing testosterone levels. This has been shown in a wide variety of situations by research studies carried out since the 1960s.[22] One of the first of these was a study I made with an Argentinean doctor, Emil Arguelles, as part of a study of the stress of airline travel.[23] He was able to show that exposure to a couple of hours of air-turbine noise in young men working in a factory was sufficient to halve their blood testosterone levels. He had already shown lowered testosterone in men following heart attacks.[24]

Moderately stressful events, such as taking exams in an army officer cadet training school, could also lower testosterone levels, though this was less pronounced in successful candidates.[25]

Even less intense stress, such as losing a tennis match where the winner would get 100 dollars, was sufficient to cause a noticeable drop in testosterone.[26] While mild to moderately intense physical stress, including intercourse, seems to increase testosterone levels, severe exertion such as running marathons was found to lower them.[27,28]

A final action of stress is to cause the release of 'stress hormones' such as adrenaline, noradrenaline and cortisol, which are breakdown 'catabolic hormones' which work against the build-up 'anabolic hormones', principally testosterone. The former raise blood sugar and fat levels and increase oxygen consumption, while the latter have the opposite action.

Alcohol

Shakespeare, in *Macbeth*, describes drink as provoking the desire, but taking away performance. This is one of the common ways in which erectile problems associated with the andropause first begin to show during middle age.

This contrasts with women, who are more susceptible to the effects of alcohol than men and yet are more sexually stimulated by it. Recent research in Sweden showed that three glasses of wine rapidly raised testosterone levels in girls in their twenties, and to a greater degree than a group of men the same age. This combination of a lessening of inhibitions and an increase in the hormone which stimulates the libido, explains the old saying, 'Candy is dandy, but liquor is quicker.' However, many women also find that it is more difficult to have an orgasm when drunk.

It is surprising how strong a poison to the testis alcohol is. It may act directly or through its immediate breakdown product, acetaldehyde[29] or by increasing SHBG.[30] Either way, even in moderate drinkers, blood testosterone levels fall as alcohol levels increase. Binge drinking to a level sufficient to cause a hangover has been found to lower testosterone levels 12 to 20 hours later – in one study to 20 per cent of their pre-party levels. Perhaps sagging hormone levels are one of the reasons why a hangover feels so awful. This might explain those eye-opening hangover cures based on boosting cholesterol levels with raw eggs.

This makes it less surprising that later in life, both because of long-term testicular damage and its short-term actions in reducing testosterone levels and erectile function, alcohol can take away both desire and performance in men. Thirty per cent of my first 400 andropausal patients reported currently drinking more than 21 units of alcohol a week and many drank two, three or four times that amount. (One unit, remember, is a half pint of beer, a glass of wine or a measure of spirit.)

The situation has recently been made worse in Europe because our heavier drinking (or more generous) partners in the EU have just raised the volume of the standard measure of spirit from 12 millilitres to 14, causing about a 17 per cent increase in the risk of damaging the testis with every glass!

Though several studies have suggested that up to 40 units of alcohol a week, especially as red wine, may protect the heart, perhaps by having both antioxidant and anti-coagulant effects, from the sexual function point of view, alcohol is generally bad news both in the short and long term. Beer and lagers appear to be particularly toxic to the testis because they contain plant oestrogens, phyto-oestrogens, from the hops and other ingredients. Even low alcohol lagers and other drinks might contain these oestrogens, and more research is needed on this important topic of international concern.

A sixteenth-century Italian physician called Cornaro wrote, 'The excesses of our youth are like drafts upon our old age, payable with interest about twenty years after date.'[31] This is certainly true in relation to alcohol. As well as those andropausal patients who were currently drinking too much, about another 10 per cent gave a past history of excess alcohol consumption for over a year or more. Unfortunately, testicular function does not seem to improve very much even if they stop drinking for several years.

This is in contrast to smoking, where most of the hazards, such as lung cancer and heart disease, decrease dramatically within five to ten years of giving up. The testis lacks the power to regenerate enjoyed by the liver and never fully recovers, as is shown by infertility, impotence and loss of libido in chronic alcoholics even after drying out. The liver forgives and forgets, but the testis remembers, so the lager louts of today are likely to be the lousy lovers of tomorrow.

The sensitivity of the testis to alcohol was clearly shown by recent studies by a research group in Milan.

They found that compared to non-drinkers, those who drank 14–21 units of alcohol per week were twice as likely to be sub-fertile and those who drank 28 units and over were nearly four times more likely.[32] This factor is well recognized in infertility clinics, particularly as a cause of poor sperm motility. It seems that unlike the men who make them, sperm just don't drink and drive.

Over-Heating

The scrotum is not a design fault by our creator to use up spare skin, as the Scottish comedian Billy Connolly insists. Nature does not risk putting vital and sensitive glands in such an exposed position without an excellent reason. This is because to function properly they need to be a few crucial degrees cooler than the rest of the body. It's as though the testis has to pluck up the courage to make a small step outside the body into the cooler scrotum and testosterone drives it to do so. This is truly a giant leap for mankind, because unless it happens, neither the desire nor the ability to father children develop. As has been mentioned previously, xeno-oestrogens, because they antagonize testosterone production and action, may have contributed to the increased incidence of non-descent seen in recent years.

This temperature question can also cause problems during and after puberty when the scrotum is increasingly kept warm by Y-front pants and tight jeans. Together, these are likely to be as bad as the padded cod-pieces which reduced the fertility of Henry VIII and his courtiers. A condition called 'varicocele' in which collections of fluid form in the scrotum and cause a warming water-jacketing effect, has also been shown to reduce testosterone levels, especially in older patients.[33]

There is an old country saying, 'Rams wrapped in wool breed no lambs.' This principle has been used by the Japanese, who have recently introduced a male contraceptive device consisting of a scrotal support with a furry nylon lining. Worn continuously, it is said to be very effective after the 2–3 month period needed to allow sperm already produced to die off.

Even mental imaging techniques, as when some university students were asked to imagine warming of the scrotum as part of their system of autogenic mental exercises, are said to have produced a marked reduction in sperm count within a couple of months.

Other studies have suggested that the polyester component of underwear may generate electromagnetic fields which impair testicular function.

The importance of testicular cooling has recently received further scientific proof in an article in the *International Journal of Andrology* by a research group in Milan, where they know a thing or two about male fashion and its penalties. Infertility was nearly twice as common in men wearing tight Y-front underpants as men wearing loose boxer shorts, and one-and-a-half times as common in men wearing tight trousers, including jeans, as loose trousers. For men who combined the two, and wore tight pants and trousers, the risk of infertility was two-and-a-half times that of those who did neither.[32]

Perhaps this principle was recognized in the past. Loose-fitting underpants made of a leather cloth soft enough not to chafe the skin were worn by Viking warriors when invading Britain 3,000 years ago, according to a recent archaeological find. However, the extremes of this advice to 'stay cool and hang loose' were seen in soldiers of the Black Watch Highland Regiment, who were forbidden to wear anything under their kilts. To enter or leave the barracks they had to walk over mirrors in the guard house, with their privates on parade, so to speak, to make sure they were obeying orders.

As testosterone production and sperm production appear, not surprisingly, to be closely linked, to promote virility as well as fertility it seems a good idea to recommend large, loose-fitting, lightweight cotton or silk boxer-type underpants. Perhaps 'Burn your Y-fronts' might be a good motto for 'men's lib'.

This explanation of the many ways in which the body's supplies of testosterone may be reduced or inactivated by the 'slings and arrows of outrageous fortune' would be incomplete without a chapter on the important part unwittingly played by doctors themselves – vasectomy.

Chapter Five

Vasectomy:
The Unkindest Cut of All

The idea that vasectomy could be a major cause of the andropause makes the many doctors who recommend it and those who inflict it on unsuspecting patients rush to its defence. Such reactions come with faith, but usually little detailed knowledge of the many possible adverse reactions to the operation.

Since it first came into fashion in the 1960s, this seemingly trivial operation has variously been described, from 'the most loving thing that a man can do for a woman' to 'the unkindest cut of all' – a 'surgical sword of Damocles' threatening the testes. It has really taken off as a means of contraception, despite the controversy, and it has been estimated that currently 500,000 Americans, 20,000 British, and 10,000 Irish men have it each year.

The first human vasectomy was performed in 1894 by a British surgeon to reduce the size of an enlarged prostate, which it apparently failed to do.[1] However, the operation never became widespread till in 1916 a Viennese surgeon, Ludwig Steinach, proclaimed it was a method of rejuvenating the male. His theory was that if the part of the testicular factory manufacturing sperm were shut down, it would leave more room for the testosterone producing cells to flourish, which would reduce ageing. The idea proved popular and on the basis of many reports from patients who claimed the operations had done wonders for them, thousands of men were 'Steinachered'. There were even reports that the illustrious father of psychoanalysis, Sigmund Freud, who also lived in Vienna, underwent the operation to promote longevity and revive his sexual powers – but perhaps this was just to overcome a psychological block.

It was also, from 1909 onwards, used as a tool in social engineering, to limit reproduction by any people considered 'defective individuals'. A particular enthusiast for this form of eugenics was a Dr Harry Sharp, resident physician at the Jeffersonville Reformatory, Indiana. He compulsorily vasectomized 280 men because they had defects of character such as 'selfishness, ingratitude, inconstancy, egotism, and inability to resist any impulse or desire' or masturbated excessively. While these traits must obviously have been very rare in the population in those days, at least in Indiana, a considerable number might now be considered as eligible on these grounds in most countries.

People on whom this form of involuntary sterilization could be inflicted ranged from colour-blind individuals to those considered undesirable because of their race or creed. From 1933 onwards, under the law 'Prevention of Hereditary Disease in Posterity' the German Government forced over a million men it considered unfit, including probably not coincidentally a large proportion of Jewish people, to undergo vasectomy.

In the USA in 1922 31 states had statutes permitting involuntary sterilization of 'defective individuals'. Even with the outcry over its abuses by the Nazis, 21 states retained these laws after the Second World War, and as recently as 1973 Tennessee, Mississippi, Ohio and Illinois introduced bills ordering the sterilization of those on welfare with two or more children. California and Oklahoma made vasectomy a condition of suspending prison sentences in those convicted of robbery or not supporting their families.[2] In Britain the Child Support Agency seems to prefer financial castration.

In India vasectomy has been vigorously promoted as a part of Government population policy. A new world record was achieved in 1971 by holding a 'Vasectomy Camp' which sterilized 63,000 men in one month. A hundred surgeons worked non-stop round the clock, while a variety of circus sideshows entertained those waiting their turn. Three years later it was revealed that gangs of 'motivators' who had been offered small sums to encourage men to undergo the operation had misled or forcibly press-ganged or blackmailed them, and nearly half the men wished they had never had it done.[3]

In Britain in 1994 an alarming increase in vasectomy rates in men in their early twenties was thought to be due to the recession and job losses making it difficult to afford the cost of housing a family. One wonders how many of these men will regret the decision.

My first experience of the clinical effects of vasectomy was in 1979 when I first visited the clinic of Dr Jens Møller in Copenhagen. A surprising number of his patients, who nearly all were being treated with testosterone for severe problems with the circulation in their legs and often heart disease as well, had had a vasectomy many years previously. When I commented on this, Dr Møller simply said, *'Ah yes. When I hear a patient has had a vasectomy, I know he is a case for me!'* This seemed at the time to be a rather extreme remark to make, but it prompted me to look up the literature on the subject.

Rather to my surprise, I found that there was a considerable amount of evidence to support Dr Møller's view that vasectomy might have harmful effects on the heart and circulation. I had not expected this, because it was such a commonly accepted operation and one which I had only just escaped having myself, in the nick of time, so to speak. It had been sold to the unsuspecting public, as it still is, as a snip. This stands for Simply No Immediate Problems. I pointed out in 1979, this is a falsely simplistic view of a complex and important issue.[4]

Let's look first at what happens during and after the operation, and then at what can and does go wrong.

Unlike any other operation, however minor, no general medical examination is done beforehand, no central records are kept of how many operations have been performed and counselling is limited to the fact that it is irreversible so be sure you want it done. No enquiries are made about previous histories of mumps or other infections which may damage the testes, or of relevant family histories of heart disease, high blood pressure or diabetes. Any questions about what happens to the sperm are brushed aside with facile answers such as 'They are just absorbed.'

In order for patients to make an informed decision about whether to take it, a drug has to have in the packaging a formidable list of every complication, however rare, ever recorded in association with the use of that compound, and often for good measure every related compound. The same should apply when an operation such as vasectomy is prescribed, but the possible complications discussed here are rarely mentioned and certainly not covered in the detail deserved. Vasectomy is, after all, a major surgical insult to a very sensitive, delicate and highly tuned organ.

Vasectomy is a deceptively simple 'minor' operation and can be, and often is, carried out by the most junior and inexperienced of surgeons. It takes quarter to half an hour and so lends itself to mass application in clinics set up for the purpose on a conveyor belt system.[5]

The actual procedure is carried out under local anaesthetic. Through a small incision, the tube carrying the sperm from the testis on each side to the prostate gland below the bladder, the *vas deferens* which gives the operation its name, is exposed. It is then dissected free of the fine nerves and blood vessels which run alongside it in the spermatic cord, and sealed off. This may be done by cutting it and tying off one or both ends, by frying it with electrocautery or by blocking it with a plastic spigot (this is claimed to be more easily reversible).

To the patient and surgeon alike it is seen as a simple plumbing job to turn off the stop-cocks and prevent sperm getting out of the testes. It is presented as a cheap and effective form of contraception, for which one is awarded a portable radio for an act of social conscience in India and a tie inscribed IOFB, standing for '*I Only Fire Blanks*', in Britain. (As the anti-vasection lobby gathers strength, refusenick members may well come to sport ties inscribed IOFLA, standing for '*I Only Fire Live Ammunition*'.)

However, after the operation there may be a variety of complications, which can be divided into short and long term. The vas itself may be damaged, as can the fine blood vessels, nerves and lymph vessels which run alongside it in the spermatic cord. These nourish the testis, control its temperature to within very critical limits and drain fluid away from it. Temperature control of the testis has been shown to be impaired after vasectomy, as has the drainage of fluid from around it so that collections of fluid called hydrocele are formed in some cases. This 'water-jacketing' tends to raise the temperature, which can have a harmful effect on the testes' ability to produce both sperm and testosterone. Not only this, but there are also nerve connections between the two testes and damage to one can affect the other in a variety of ways.

There is often mild to moderate discomfort which may cause the patient to be off work for anything from an hour to a week, depending on his pain threshold, motivation and how many of the fine nerve endings that run alongside the vas get caught up in the operation.

Fortunately quite infrequently, a variety of other changes can occur which cause a persistent and disabling 'post-vasectomy pain syndrome'.[6,7] If both ends of the vas have been tied off, the pressure in the stump attached to the testis builds up, and sometimes cysts form in the sperm-collecting tubules surrounding the testis. They can be felt as small lumps. Sometimes the cysts burst open and swellings at the severed ends of the vas arise called granulomas. They are due to a local tissue reaction to sperm. If the vas has been left open, then the sperm spill out into the loose tissue in the scrotum, and granulomas are then more likely to form than cysts.

In either case, but particularly where granulomas have formed, the body reacts to this highly unnatural no-exit situation by becoming allergic to its own sperm and producing anti-sperm antibodies. This is because sperm are only produced after puberty and are normally kept shielded from the body's immune system. This would otherwise attack them, reacting just as it would to other 'alien' proteins such as those produced by bacteria and viruses. Vasectomy spills sperm into the tissues around the testis and exposes them to the antibody producing cells.[8]

You only have to meet a few of these post-vasectomy pain syndrome cases to be far more cautious about recommending the operation. One of these cases is Harry:

I had my vasectomy 10 years ago now and I haven't had a happy, pain-free day since. It's been a nightmare from beginning to end and it's not over yet.

After seven years on the pill, my wife was advised to stop taking it and so I decided I'd have a vasectomy. On the day of the operation at our local hospital I had no second thoughts at all because I had heard that the procedure was quite straightforward. I was surprised therefore to wake from the general anaesthetic with a tremendous pain in my stomach. The nurse reassured me the pain would go away and gave me valium. But when my friend arrived to take me home an hour later, I was still bent double with pain.

After a couple of days with no respite, I called in my own doctor who confirmed that it would settle down. But for the next few weeks I was only comfortable when I was lying down. Walking or lifting things was impossible and there was no question of being able to work. I was getting increasingly anxious as I had never really been ill before, but since both the hospital and my doctor were adamant there was nothing to worry about, I was prepared to give it time.

Then two months after the operation I found two small and painful lumps in each testicle. I was told these were sperm granulomas, the sperm not being properly ab- sorbed into the body, and was shocked when the consultant told me he wasn't experienced in dealing with such problems and wanted to refer me to another hospital. By the time this appointment came up, the lumps had grown from being the size of match heads to the size of peas and they, together with the continuing ache in my stomach region, were causing me such discomfort that it was interfering with my whole life.

The new consultant performed an operation to remove the

lumps. Afterwards he told me he believed too much of the vas had been cut away during the vasectomy, which explained the painful pulling sensation in my stomach, and I felt very angry. The lumps kept recurring and this was complicated by bouts of urinary infection that caused a painful inflammation in both testicles. To help this the surgeon finally had to remove the inflamed outer casing of the left testicle, the epididymis. Even this went wrong. Five months later the testis on that side began to shrink, and I had to have it removed and a plastic prosthesis put in.

By now I felt extremely low and tired and couldn't understand why. Some tests done down in London showed a very low testosterone level and that I was so allergic to my own sperm that even when they diluted my blood more than 2,000 times they could still get an anti-sperm reaction.

I was originally given some tablets called Proviron and these made me feel slightly better, though it took testosterone injections to make me feel much fitter. But even these wore off after a time. Last year I had to have the same series of operations on my right testicle, with removal of a granuloma, and then the epididymis, and now the testicle gets inflamed and is shrinking, so I may have to have even that removed.

It's been such a terrible time since the first operation. My job as a fork-lift truck driver, which I'd had for 18 years before the vasectomy, is gone, and my wife left me because it all got too much and we weren't having any fun or any sex. There have been times over the last few years when the pain and worry have made me think of ending it all, but things are slightly better now.

All this has been a result of a vasectomy gone wrong, probably because it was performed in a hurry by someone inexperienced, though I'm told it sometimes happens in the best of hands. This surgery sentenced me to 10 years' pain and misery.

Long-term complications of vasectomy may be much

more common and diverse than is generally recognized. Of the limited amount of research which has been done, some is reassuring and some rather worrying.

Apart from causing infertility problems in patients wanting the vasectomy reversed, which happens in 1 per cent, no one seems to have thought through the other likely consequences. It's like tying a knot in the barrel of a rifle and being surprised when it blows back in your face!

I have been carrying out detailed antibody profiles in the post-vasectomy patients who have come to see me. There are some interesting but inconsistent findings which I am now analysing in detail.

Some of my patients reported a prolonged and debilitating 'flu-like illness within the first few months after vasectomy, which is when immune reactions would be expected, and granulomas appear.

Some patients show an active generalized immune process as shown by raised levels in the blood of a protein called 'immune complement' which has been linked to the possibility of increased heart and circulatory disease after vasectomy.

The majority show anti-sperm antibodies. In fact it has been widely recognized and accepted for many years that anti-sperm antibodies are found in up to three-quarters of vasectomized men. One medical researcher on the subject cheerfully says, *'Vasectomy can be considered a particular form of experimental autoimmunization.'*[9]

An interesting and as far I know unexplained sex difference is apparent here. When women develop anti-sperm antibodies, these usually cause the sperm to clump together 'head to head', whereas the majority of my post-vasectomy men seem to have 'tail to tail' antibodies, sometimes active when their plasma is diluted

over 16,000 times. Logic suggests that if you have antibodies against sperm, you might well develop antibodies
against sperm-producing cells in the testis, the Sertoli or
nurse cells, and indeed this is found in a proportion of
cases.[10,11]

What was not expected was the finding in other
cases of antibodies against the testosterone producing,
interstitial cells, though this again seems logical. The
sperm and testosterone producing cells work together,
literally side by side, on the common mission of
producing and launching these 'egg-seeking missiles'.
Recent research has shown just how closely these functions are linked in many ways, including their own
hormonal communications, the so-called paracrine
actions.[12] If you suddenly shut down one half of the
factory, common sense would indicate that you might
have some effect on the other. From my research and
that of others, including testicular biopsies from vasectomized men, there is evidence that this is indeed the
case.

Vasectomy and the Andropause

Over the last 10 years, I have been impressed by the fact
that nearly 250 out of the 1,000 men in my practice
complaining of symptoms of the andropause have had
vasectomies.

It is difficult to get accurate reports on the proportion
of men in different countries who have had vasectomies
because the operation is assumed safe and thought too
trivial to be worth recording. However, as the best esti-
mate of the frequency of vasectomy in British men of
this age and social group is between 5 and 10 per cent,
there seems to be a significantly higher proportion of
men who have had this operation in the andropausal

group. Not only are these patients on average five years younger than the rest, but often this operation appears to be the only risk factor present.

The most common time for the symptoms to appear is 10 to 15 years after the vasectomy. This time scale was confirmed independently by another group in London, who also showed a fall in testosterone levels at this time.[13] Other studies from Egypt and Belgium have shown that the amount of testosterone and one of its active fractions, dihydrotestosterone (DHT), in the semen are reduced to one third by vasectomy.

Most of the studies of the effects of vasectomy on hormone production are relatively short term, being over three to five years at most.[14] Almost all were carried out 10 to 20 years ago, before vital factors such as sex hormone binding globulin (SHBG) and prostate specific antigen (PSA) were being included in even research studies. It's true they excluded any dramatic drop in total testosterone levels in the first five years after vasectomy, and some even showed an increase in DHT and follicle stimulating hormone (FSH).[15,16,17] However this indicates at least some hormonal changes occur even in this relatively short time scale, which could be taken to show some disturbance in testicular function, if not actual damage to its structure. Rather than vasectomy making you sexier, as suggested by one study recently, since DHT is not the primary hormone governing libido, a more likely explanation is that the pituitary gland is trying to compensate for impaired testosterone production by spurring the testis to greater activity, and increasing its turnover rate.

The surge in these two hormones could also explain why there have been several reports[18,19,20] of an increased number of cases of testicular cancer within the first four years after vasectomy, reaching a maximum after two, though there are other studies which contradict this.[21] This tumour is increasing at a rate of about 2 per cent per annum, particularly in young men. It is more common when the testicles fail to descend, or they are damaged by mumps or trauma,[22] which is a condition also associated with raised FSHs. It has recently been linked to environmental oestrogens, which, as already mentioned, may have a similar effect in contributing to testicular failure and high FSH levels.[23] It is fortunate that this is one form of cancer where great advances have been made in treatment.

Another form of cancer which has been linked to vasectomy in some studies but not in others is that of the prostate.[24,25] Evidence is particularly conflicting here, but again, if it is proven, it could be explained by long-term hormonal disturbances. Reduced semen flow through the prostate has been suggested as another possible link, but seems unlikely, as vasectomy only reduces semen volume by 5 per cent, and this form of cancer is not particularly common in men leading a celibate life, such as monks.

Typical of the andropausal men I have seen where vasectomy seemed to be the most likely cause of their problems is the 49-year-old doctor Alan:

I had my vasectomy 10 years ago. It was very painful and I had a lot of bruising. Suddenly, for no apparent reason, five years ago the bottom dropped out of my sex life. I used to be quite a flirt but then the sexual chemistry went and sex never entered my head, which was totally unlike me. About the same time, quite suddenly my morning erections disappeared and soon the evening ones went out of the door with them, especially when I wanted them most. This made me so worried that, a bit like my golf swing, which worsened at the same time, I got paralysis by analysis.

Also, while I used to really fizz all the time, I became a real slouch, stopped going to parties and started feeling old before my time. Then the circulation in my fingers and toes got quite bad even in the mild weather, and my feet started going numb. Even my joints started seizing up and got very stiff first thing in the morning and after golf or going running, both of which I used to enjoy, but they turned into a real bore and chore with all these symptoms.

At this stage I went and had a thorough check-up by my andrologist, who showed that the free testosterone in my blood was very much reduced. Capsules of testosterone by mouth gave a lot of improvement, but it wasn't until I started on the pellet implants into the buttock that the symptoms really went away and I got back to my old sexy self.

Best of all, my golf improved enormously. My handicap, which had deteriorated badly over the previous four years, went down by about five, and I started to beat the club champion and do well in away matches. The main difference was in my swing, which had become hasty and snatched, but on testosterone really flowed. Other people noticed the difference, especially my coach, and asked what I was on, but I haven't told them. I don't think it's my imagination either, because every five or six months when my implant is running down, my golf gets worse, as does my temper and sex life, and they are only restored by another shot of testosterone.

Especially when there are other causes of testicular failure, such as alcohol or mumps, vasectomy definitely seems to lower the age at which andropausal symptoms appear.

Vasectomy, the Heart and Circulatory Disease

A great deal of work has been done on the possible link between vasectomy and heart and circulatory disease, and I find the evidence persuasive. It also coincides with my clinical experience and that of Dr Jens Møller and his successor Dr Michael Hansen.[26] It's true that a lot of the evidence implicating vasectomy in these conditions is from animal studies, but much of it is from experiments with monkeys, which are generally considered the closest one can get to the human condition.

Over 20 years ago it was shown that baboons given a high fat diet and inoculated with antibody producing proteins developed more arterial disease.[27] A few years after that the American queen of research in this field, Dr Nancy Alexander, and her colleague Dr Clarkson showed that diet-induced arterial disease developed more in vasectomized cynomolgus monkeys than in sham-operated controls. They therefore suggested, 'The immunological response to sperm antigens that often accompanies vasectomy may exacerbate atherosclerosis.' This is the form of arterial degeneration underlying most coronary heart disease.[28]

They followed up this early work with longer term studies which showed even more marked changes. This was largely confirmed in studies on primates by several other groups of researchers, particularly where the monkeys were overfed and underexercised, like the average Western male.

Though the link in monkeys between vasectomy and arterial disease is very clearly established, that in humans is much less so. Some studies, such as the Framingham study of heart disease risk factors in America, found an association with higher cholesterol levels, and one, on Korean men, higher heart attack rates.[29,30] Others, such as the Oxford Record Linkage study and a Kaiser Permanente study in California, did not.[21,31] The debate continues and the case has yet to be proved either way.

As well as the antibody related theories, there are a variety of reasons why vasectomy might contribute to circulatory problems. **Anything which reduces the production of testosterone or antagonizes its actions is likely to contribute to these conditions. Dr Møller lists the reasons fully in his book** *Testosterone Treatment of Circulatory Diseases.*" **Mainly it is because of imbalance between the body's anabolic building up, restorative, energy producing activities and its catabolic, breaking down, energy consuming activities. As a result, the blood pressure and fat levels rise, blood clots happen more easily, flow of blood in the small blood vessel becomes sluggish, and the cells throughout the body become less efficient at taking up oxygen and using it. Consequently the natural rate of wear and tear on the heart and arteries escalates, and this leads to their premature ageing.**

The most dramatic case I saw where vasectomy seemed to be directly linked with circulatory problems was James, a young milkman from south London:

I was fine till I was 21 and then I got the mumps. It was so bad that my testicles swelled to the size of grapefruit, and I had to borrow a bra from my mum to carry them and ease the pain when I stood up. They seemed to settle down all right after an uncomfortable couple of weeks, but there must have been some damage because my wife had difficulty conceiving our first child and the clinic said my sperm count was low.

We made up for lost time, though, after that and had two more quickly, so I thought it was time to have a vasectomy. There was a little counselling beforehand, but no medical checks, as I looked and felt completely fit, and was only 34. No one asked me about the mumps, so I didn't think it could be relevant. The operation went fine and within a week I was back to my old sexy self, or even better.

Ten months later, though, I didn't feel nearly so good. I found that on my milk rounds, especially on cold winter mornings, I started getting really bad cramps in first my right calf and then my left. I was hobbling up the garden paths like an old man, and my rounds started taking longer and longer. I told my GP about this and he said these symptoms sounded like not enough blood was getting to the leg muscles, but he had never seen this in anyone so young before.

The surgeon he sent me to was also very puzzled. He said surgery was needed, but I didn't fancy it and tried to treat myself by stopping smoking and exercising in a gym. This helped for a bit, but within a year I had to give in and have some of the furring up in the main artery in the right leg taken out.

This only helped for a couple of months and then I was back in hospital having a whole series of complicated plumbing operations, trying to bypass the blockages with plastic tubes. None of these operations lasted more than a month or two and I couldn't do my rounds even when I was out of hospital because of the leg cramps. It got to the point of getting cramp in my right leg at night in bed and the surgeons started talking about amputation.

I was desperate and would rather have committed suicide than live life as a legless cripple. Still, I'm a philosophical sort of man who meditates and I still believed something would happen to save my legs. Well, I was lying in a bed on the surgical ward one morning going through The Sunday Times and there was this article about a Dr Møller in Copenhagen who was treating cases like mine with testosterone injections. Fate seemed to have been very kind to me, because a British doctor who was mentioned in the same article and seemed to believe in the treatment was working in the hospital just across the road from where I was.

He and my surgeon got together and agreed it was worth a try. After all, what had I got to lose, apart from my legs? Dr Carruthers really had to fight for the injections. Though my surgeon had given his permission, the hospital pharmacist said he thought the dose suggested was far too high and, among other dire warnings, that it might suppress my sperm produc-tion, which showed how little he knew about my case. This made the junior doctor who was told to give the injections, as no one else would, so nervous that he spilt half the dose out of the syringe each time.

Even so, it really was amazing. A few days after I started on the twice a week injections, my legs seemed to come alive again. The calf pain started taking longer and longer to come on, and I was able to leave the ward and take up my milk rounds, which badly needed my attention. One improvement I hadn't expected was that my erections returned nearly to normal after being very lame affairs for a couple of years and I was only slightly tired for a couple of days after sex rather than being shattered for a week.

There was a setback a couple of months later when the old plastic piping the surgeons had left in my right leg got infected and had to be taken out. This briefly made the blood flow in my right foot very bad indeed, so that gangrene nearly set in, but despite this, things went very well on the injections. My family doctor arranged for me to have them twice a week. I gave up going to the hospital, which seemed to lose interest in me when I didn't need any more surgery, and I wasn't sorry to stay out of their hands.

It's now six years since I started the testosterone treatment and I work out in a gym for an hour most days, swim twice a week, enjoy a great sex life and, having given up the stressful job of being a milkman, I am much happier teaching Tai Chi.

The funny thing is, though, none of the surgeons I used to consult seemed interested in why things went wrong so soon after the vasectomy or why I'm not in a wheelchair now, six years after they said amputation was the only option left.

Most of the research studies on human vasectomy are unfortunately relatively short term, lasting only two to five years and ceasing before the complications I see 10 to 15 years later arise. One of the best conducted and reassuring studies was reported from Oxford in 1992. It found that:

> *Vasectomy was not associated with an increased risk of testicular cancer or the other diseases studied. With respect to prostate cancer, while we found no cause for concern, longer periods of observation on large numbers of men are required.*[14]

However this study did not cover impaired sexual function and other symptoms of the andropause. Also, it is difficult when seeing case after case of severe menopausal and circulatory disease problems which appear to be directly associated with vasectomy to be entirely convinced of its safety by the statistics of very artificial population studies.

Also, the vasectomized men are likely to be a very atypical self-selected group of clean living, well informed, health-conscious men in stable and loving relationships, who might be expected to enjoy better health all round, and yet are being compared with control populations who may lack these benefits.

Vested Interests

There are powerful lobbies both inside and outside the medical profession with vested interests in maintaining the 'safe' image of vasectomy. First, doctors who have been promoting it for many years don't want to change their tune and to have to face the possibility of being in the wrong.

I saw this very clearly in 1979 when, alarmed by the similarities between Dr Møller's experience with his men and the evidence from the research in monkeys, I encouraged a very well informed and level-headed medical correspondent for a popular national newspaper to write an article analysing the vasectomy dilemma. Having done his homework very thoroughly, to the extent of visiting Dr Møller's clinic in Copenhagen, he stated in his article: *'The view I have reached can be summarized as follows: with the present state of knowledge, I wouldn't dream of having a vasectomy myself.'* His conclusion was: 'It's safer to wait.'[4]

Though this article was cautious by journalistic standards, there was an immediate outcry by the medical establishment. The British Pregnancy Advisory Service dismissed the report as *'scare-mongering'* and other experts the journalist had consulted to get a balanced view before publication asked him not to write about it at all.

I was involved in several radio and television debates on the question at the time, and the main argument of the antagonistic doctors was that vasectomy operations had been carried out for about a century and there had never been reports of an association between vasectomy and atherosclerosis in man. Would they have dismissed such evidence of arterial damage in monkeys, if it had been produced by a drug rather than an operation? It is more likely there would have been a public outcry and the drug would have been taken off the market pending further research.

All this fierce opposition was before questions raised by the possibility of a link to testicular or prostatic cancer or to the hormonal disturbances involved in the andropause. The steadfast support of the pro-vasectomy lobby was undeterred even by this possibility.

This reluctance of the medical profession to discuss vasectomy issues is likely to be even greater when the financial considerations of the vasectomy industry are taken into account.

In America, for example, it is estimated that 500,000 vasectomies are being carried out each year. Assuming that on average, with operative fees and all the associated costs such as testing for the absence of sperm three months after the operation, the cost of each vasectomy is $400, that is an annual turnover of $200 million. Add in another $15 million for the 1 per cent of men who want the operation reversed at $3,000 dollars each, and a similar amount for treating the other short-term complications such as infection, pain, cysts, granulomas and so on, and this is quite a big business, well worth protecting.

There is, however, one consideration which might give American doctors in particular cause for thought before they continue to recommend and perform vasectomies. If convincing evidence were produced that serious damage might result from either the antibody formation or hormonal changes which many studies have already shown to occur after the operation, it would open the floodgates for a torrent of highly emotive litigation cases. Even now, drug companies are having to defend some very large-scale group actions for everything from breast implants to drugs such as Thalidomide and Norplant.

In the brochure selling vasectomy in one large clinic in London the details are very brief, and so incomplete and inaccurate as to flout advertising standards, let alone medical guidelines for informed consent to treatment. There are four brief paragraphs on possible hazards of the operation, which I quote in their entirety so that you can form your own impression as to whether this is full and fair advice:

Complications, although very rare, can occur with any surgical procedure, however minor, and if you are worried about anything please feel free to call us for advice, or alternatively, if it is convenient, your own GP.

There is no evidence of any long-term risk to men's health after vasectomy, in fact many couples find greater enjoyment once the risk of unwanted pregnancy has been removed. Orgasm and ejaculation are not affected.

Sperm continues to be produced by the testicles but its passage to the penis is blocked, so it is reabsorbed by the body, just as the body continually re-absorbs all unused cells.

Vasectomy has absolutely no effect on the production of male hormones, the only difference is purely mechanical in that the semen no longer contains sperm.

Continuing with this limited 'purely mechanical' view, the form the patient completes before the operation usually has more room for payment details than medical details.

Often immediately after signing this form, the man, who may be only in his twenties or thirties, is led off, without even the time to reconsider which he would have if he were buying a washing machine, to have an operation with possible life-long complications of which he knows little, performed by a doctor of whom he knows less. Lawyers defending such cases in the future may have a hard time proving that the individual or organizations performing vasectomies under these conditions were acting responsibly towards their patients.

It's not only doctors who don't want to hear any bad news about vasectomy, though – governments also see it as the cheap and simple answer to population control. This was seen in March 1991 in the House of Lords, when Lord Anthony Blyth asked Her Majesty's Government *'whether they will take steps to discourage the vasectomy operation in view of the possible harmful effects in the long term'*.

The Minister answering on behalf of the Government, Lord Henley, immediately said:

*No, my Lords. The decision as to whether or not a vasectomy should be performed in any particular case is one for the patient and doctor concerned, **taking full account of all the clinical issues involved. The patient is entitled to have sufficient information on which to make a balanced judgement**. It is for the doctor, as part of the counselling process, to decide what risks, **if any**, the patient should be warned of and the terms in which any warning should be given.* (My bold italics).

Under further questioning the Minister confirmed that the Government was satisfied that men were indeed being given adequate advice, discounted the studies associating vasectomy with testicular or prostatic cancer and omitted to mention any of the studies relating to circulatory disease.

Another Lord was of the opinion:

If there was any evidence of harmful effects from this comparatively minor operation, whether in the short or long term, should not the Chief Medical Officer of the Department [of Health] inform general practitioners of that fact? As he has not taken that step, am I entitled to assume that there are no such dangers?

The Minister confirmed he was.

I entirely agree with critics who say that the evidence

against vasectomy is not conclusive yet and much more research is needed. However, as elsewhere in this book, discussion of the topic has deliberately been made provocative to stimulate research and informed debate. Particularly in relation to the andropause, those who have had vasectomies should not be unduly alarmed, because symptoms generally respond very well to testosterone treatment. However, sometimes higher doses seem needed in this situation and, because the antibody changes are not reversible, treatment may need to be prolonged.

Also, unless it is needed to restore fertility, reversal of the vasectomy is not recommended. This might even stir up a fresh storm of antibody production. It is also quite an expensive operation and there are only a few surgeons who have the expertise needed for this delicate form of microsurgery, which even in the most experienced hands has its own range of post-operative complications.

Vasectomy is a common operation and even if short-term complications only occur in a small proportion of people, or it has just a slight influence on the long-term chances of developing a serious illness such as prostate cancer,[35] this makes it important that we learn much more about it, and that people who have had it done, or are considering it, are better informed.[36]

The first recorded vasectomy was by a British surgeon, Sir Astley Cooper, who in 1823 vasectomized his dog.[37] My clinical experience over the past 15 years has made me firmly of the opinion that it shouldn't even happen to a dog. If you or a friend are thinking of having the knot of vasectomy tied, my earnest advice to you would be: Don't!

Having answered at least some of the questions about

how the male menopause or andropause happens, and the part which vasectomy may play, it's time to find out the good news: that it can usually be safely and effectively treated by giving testosterone.

Chapter Six

Testosterone Replacement Therapy (TRT)

TRT is but one of a broad range of methods for preventing and treating the andropause. Often, however, it proves the key to the door to recovery and puts men in a more positive frame of mind to undertake the other necessary steps, such as managing stress, drinking less, losing weight and exercising.

Before deciding whether TRT is suitable and what additional treatments are needed to maximize its effects, the physician prescribing it will need to undertake a detailed 'work up'. When you go to him, first your health history should be taken carefully and fully. Factors which might have damaged the testes or stopped them functioning properly, such as non-descent, inflammations or orchitis such as mumps, vasectomy and other traumas, and local anatomical abnormalities must be discussed.

Then there needs to be an 'Andropause Checklist' similar to the one given in the second chapter *(see pages 66–7)*. This will establish whether you have the symptoms which could be attributed to the andropause and how severe they are, as well as giving a baseline against which the effects of treatment can be measured.

Next comes a lifestyle and stress assessment questionnaire, which assesses the health history and lifestyle factors such as alcohol intake, diet, exercise, relaxation, smoking habits and stress related factors.

After this comes a physical check, with special emphasis on the heart and arteries, testicles and penis, and a digital rectal examination of the prostate gland. For those over 50, it is advisable to have a transrectal ultrasound examination of the prostate in addition to the mandatory prostate specific antigen (PSA) blood test which is the best overall early warning system for prostate cancer and an essential screening test before considering treatment with testosterone. The ultrasound examination is, however, quite expensive and seldom popular and newer advances in PSA testing measuring total and free forms of PSA may make it necessary less often.

The case for early detection of prostate cancer is still being fiercely debated. In my first 1,000 patients, six cases of early non-invasive prostate cancer were found prior to testosterone treatment and only one developed it during treatment, when it was picked up by the six-monthly repeat screens at an early, treatable stage. In both cases this is a lower incidence than would be expected in a group of men with the majority over 50 and would suggest that, by providing the benefit of this careful repeated screening, testosterone treatment is overall more likely to save lives from prostate cancer than to cause it.

Finally, a detailed fasting blood profile, including a hormone profile, full biochemistry with checks on the liver, kidneys, blood fats and sugar, and haematological measurements of the red and white cells, is carried out in the laboratory. The hormone measurements include the total testosterone and the SHBG, the protein in the blood which limits its action, from which, as already given, the active fraction, the free androgen index (FAI), can be calculated by dividing the first by the second and multiplying by 100 to give a percentage. This key factor should normally be in the range 70 to 100 per cent and andropausal symptoms are almost always present when it falls below 50 per cent.

For reasons already mentioned *(see pages 88–9)*, while the total testosterone level is often normal, even if in the lower part of the range, the FAI is usually significantly reduced before treatment and is the most reliable hormonal marker of the andropause. No assessment of a man with symptoms which might be related to the andropause is complete without it.

Also measured in the hormone profile are the two pituitary gland hormones which stimulate the testes, the follicle stimulating hormone (FSH) and luteinizing hormone (LH). For the reasons again already described *(see page 83)*, the former, against textbook theory, is usually raised more than the latter in many, but not all, cases of the andropause.[2]

Another important hormone which should be included on the initial screen is one from the pituitary gland, prolactin, which, as its name suggests, in women stimulates breast milk production. It also acts as a natural contraceptive, reducing fertility while women are breastfeeding and helping to space out pregnancies. It may be raised in both sexes during periods of stress, which reduces fertility and can lower testosterone production in the male.

Rarely, there is a benign tumour of the pituitary called a prolactinoma, which produces large amounts of this hormone, and testosterone levels fall dramatically. This results in loss of libido and potency, and all the other signs of testosterone deficiency. One positive benefit of the detailed hormonal profiling carried out in all cases before starting testosterone treatment is that these tumours are detected at an early stage, before other side-effects of the pituitary enlargement, such as headaches and impaired vision due to pressure on the optic nerves, are felt. Fortunately, in the five cases seen in my first 1,000 patients, their symptoms were dramatically relieved by an anti-prolactin drug called bromocriptin, which also shrank the enlarged pituitary gland back to a normal size and avoided neurosurgery.

One of the oestrogen group of hormones, oestradiol (E2), is also included in the blood test and sometimes gives interesting information. Since it is produced in men mainly by the metabolism of testosterone, where that is in short supply it often goes down. When the patient is overweight, there is a tendency for more of the natural testosterone, and even that given as treatment, to be converted to E2, and this may then rise to a level where it causes breast enlargement and may also reduce the action of the parent hormone. This paradoxical reaction only seems to happen in a few patients. It can be reduced by a variety of changes in the treatment given, as some forms of testosterone are not converted to E2. There is also scope for investigating the use of the newer forms of anti-oestrogen drugs, which are proving very effective in the treatment of breast cancer in women and show promise as an additional weapon in the treatment of andropausal men.[3,4]

Unfortunately, as yet there is no convenient blood test for the oestrogen mimics, xeno-oestrogens, or the anti-androgens already discussed, which may be playing a part in bringing on the andropause. Such a test would be a great boon to mankind, both in relation to this condition and falling sperm counts.[5]

133

When the results of all these tests are in, which can usually be done within a day if you are eager to get started, then a second session is needed with your doctor. At this you go over the results together and draw up an overall treatment programme. This is usually not just giving testosterone, but also involves active input on your part, modifying your lifestyle in a variety of ways, reducing weight and alcohol intake, moving to boxer shorts and adopting stress-coping strategies if necessary.

Always remember, *you* are in the pilot's seat and in overall control of your life. In relation to testosterone treatment, having had the risks and likely benefits explained and your questions clearly answered, you have to decide whether to have the treatment, and literally call the shots.

TRT can be given in the form of injections, pills, pellets and through the skin as creams and patches. The decision whom to treat, with which preparation in what doses and for how long, must rest with the individual physician, as part of a joint and informed venture with the patient. Here I can only give my personal experience, my views derived from it and a review of the extensive literature on the subject.

Though when asked where the testosterone comes from, doctors sometimes tell patients that it is extracted from Peruvian bulls' testicles in the mating season, both to explain the cost of the treatment and maximize the placebo effect, that's a lot of bull really. In actual fact the testosterone is made synthetically from cholesterol, the same raw material as the body uses to produce it. The cost of these preparations at present is usually roughly two to three times that of equivalent oestrogen preparations used for female HRT, but hopefully as TRT is used more often, drug companies will be able to reduce this sex hormone discrimination against men.

When testosterone was first produced back in 1935 it was realized that being poorly absorbed and rapidly broken down in the liver, it would not be effective when taken by mouth. So it was necessary to both by-pass the liver and to chemically modify the molecule to slow its rate of absorption and breakdown. One of the most effective ways was to attach side chains to the testosterone molecule and form compounds called esters. The longer the side chain in general, the slower the rate of breakdown.[6] But how to administer it?

Injections

Injections of pure testosterone were tried early on, but were found to work for only two hours. Though the effects were good while they lasted, some means had to be found of getting a longer period of action if the treatment was to become popular.

The first attempt at this was by making an ester called testosterone propionate. Having a short side chain, it only lasted two or three days, but this enabled it to be used clinically, even if it meant injections two or three times a week. This was the preparation used in 1944 by Heller and Myers *(see pages 23–7)* to demonstrate for once, if not for all, that the male menopause is due to testosterone deficiency. They also showed, in a controlled trial using placebo injections of sesame oil, how the symptoms of this very real hormonal disorder, including erection problems, could be abolished by TRT.[7]

After the Second World War, research on finding newer and more effective preparations got under way. An ester called testosterone enanthate (Primo-Teston Depot) was produced by the Schering company in

Berlin and found to be clinically very effective. Having a longer side chain, it was broken down even more slowly and injections lasted two or three weeks.

It was this preparation which Dr Jens Møller used with such impressive results in his clinic in Copenhagen for over 30 years in treating circulatory disorders.[8] It was given in high doses of 250 mg once or even in severe cases twice a week. As in the case of James *(see pages 120–23)*, it usually gives a dramatic relief of symptoms within a few days.

It is also the best injectable form widely available in the USA at present and produced excellent results in a 'Hormonal Healthcare Centre' I established and was medical director of in Hawaii. The patients I saw there showed just the same symptoms as the ones coming for treatment to London and it seems that the andropause can strike with equal force even in the 'Paradise Islands'.

There are other esters available, and cocktail mixtures of esters such as the commonly used Sustenon, but they seem to have no advantage over testosterone enanthate. They all share the problem of giving a peak of testosterone after a few hours which is higher than needed and might have some harmful effects, for example on the liver. The surplus can also be converted to oestrogen, which is again undesirable. The level then falls steadily over a week or two to a trough which may be insufficient to relieve the andropausal or circulatory symptoms. The patient is aware of these ups and downs of the testosterone levels, and his life can be a roller-coaster ride of emotional and sexual highs and lows. Also the injections, usually given into the buttock, are somewhat painful and quite expensive, which limit their availability and popularity, especially for long-term use.

To overcome some of these disadvantages, several

very promising new injections are now undergoing clinical trials. They offer the possibility of an extended action lasting between two and four months per shot. This would also get round the problems of poor and variable absorption of the oral forms, where 50 to 80 per cent of this expensive hormone goes down the toilet, the problem of fluctuating blood levels and the natural dislike of most men to taking medicine two or three times a day, perhaps for years on end.

Pills

It was a tragedy for testosterone treatment that the first oral form to be produced back in 1935 was methyl testosterone. As already explained, it was effective but had some very dangerous side-effects which have tarnished the medical image of testosterone to this day. Even though we now have much safer preparations, it can be obtained over the counter, without prescription, in many parts of the Far East and is still the only oral form of testosterone available in the United States. Why is that watchdog of American medicine, the Federal Drug Administration (FDA), still asleep in allowing this drug onto the market, while keeping the much better and safer varieties of this vital hormone out?

The harmful side-effects of methyl testosterone include damage to the liver cells, resulting in cysts and even cancer. Unlike other forms of testosterone, it also sends up blood fat levels, particularly cholesterol. This is why one of the doctors who is a leading authority on testosterone, Professor Eberhard Nieschlag from Munich, firmly stated in his 1990 review of different forms of testosterone treatment:

Because of the side-effects methyl testosterone should no

*longer be used therapeutically, in particular since effective
alternatives are available. The German Endocrine Society
declared methyl testosterone obsolete in 1981 and the
German Federal Health Authority ruled that methyl
testosterone should be withdrawn from the market in
1988. In other countries, however, methyl testosterone is
still in use, a practice which should be terminated.*[9]

These are strong words indeed, but ones with which I
entirely agree.

The dangers of this compound being foisted on a
largely unsuspecting public were vividly brought home
to me recently by the story of an engineer called Ken
who had been forced to go overseas to get his testosterone supplies:

*At the tender age of 37 I started to feel a severe lack of energy
and lost interest in everything. Life just seemed too much
bother. My work as a service engineer involved new techniques
using computers and I started only just being able to keep
up with the rapidly advancing technology, instead of being
ahead of it as I had been before. This and my reduced libido
and increasing difficulty with erections all combined to
make me feel mildly depressed and generally flat. Even my
physique started to deteriorate, and playing squash, or even
carrying a heavy toolbox up stairs, began to make me puff
and pant.*

*After trying all sorts of things from hypnosis to acupuncture
and herbal remedies for three years, I went to my family doctor,
who checked me over. After a blood test he said my testosterone
was below normal, but said he didn't advise any treatment.
When I persisted, he got quite irritable and said, 'Well, your
work takes you round the world a lot – why don't you get some
on your travels?'*

*At the time I was spending alternate months in Thailand, so
on my very next trip I went into a drug store over there, where*

you can get about anything over the counter with no questions asked, and got some 'Metesto'. The label on the bottle said that each white tablet contained 25 mg of Methyltestosterone, made in Bangkok, so it sounded like just what I needed. The instructions were in Thai, so as there were 100 tablets in the bottle and I wanted them to last a month, I decided that one three times a day would be the right dose and away I went.

I must say, within a few days I began to feel much better, quite my old self. My wife said I looked better when I got home at the end of the month, but the job in Thailand finished and when the pills ran out, all the old symptoms came back.

This time I went to a specialist in the field, who after detailed tests said my testosterone was now only a tenth of what it should be, and the form of testosterone I'd taken had caused some hopefully temporary liver damage and raised my blood cholesterol. He put me on a safer preparation also taken by mouth and within three months I was feeling fine again, and my liver function and cholesterol were back down to normal.

Now, two years later, I'm having pellet implants of testosterone, which keep me feeling very well and fit. The funny thing is that my wife, who is going through the menopause and couldn't keep up with my libido, which has returned to what it was before my problems started, is having just a touch of testosterone in with her oestrogen pellet implants, so that we have ended up on the same medicine.

There are two much safer oral preparations available in Britain and the rest of Europe, South Africa and Australia, and I have used them both extensively over the past seven years in treating patients with symptoms of the andropause.

The stronger of the two preparations is a long chain fatty acid ester called testosterone undecanoate, first used clinically in the mid 1970s. It is known under the trade names given to it by the Belgian company Organon which makes it: Restandol in Europe and Andriol in the rest of the world, including Canada where it has only recently come onto the market. It is made in small reddish-brown oval capsules containing 40 mg of the ester, equivalent to 25 mg of testosterone. It is dissolved in arachis oil so that when taken after a meal it is absorbed by the fat droplets coming from the small intestine, goes into the lymphatic drainage and by-passes the liver so that it is not immediately broken down. Peak serum levels are reached after two to four hours and most is broken down by eight hours, so that this form needs to be taken two or ideally three times a day.

The other safe oral preparation is mesterolone (Proviron), which comes in the form of white 25 mg tablets made by the German firm Schering. Unlike testosterone itself and other testosterone derivatives, which are broken down to both an active product called dihydrotestosterone (DHT) and oestrogens, mesterolone only produces raised levels of the former, which makes it a weaker androgen, particularly in relation to improving both libido and potency. However, for unknown reasons, it still sometimes seems to work when the undecanoate fails and so is a useful reserve form, especially when it is wished to maintain or even improve fertility, which the other preparations may temporarily suppress. It can, for instance, help young men with the *'locker room syndrome'* described in Chapter Eight to feel more 'macho'. An example of this type of case is Nick:

Though I'm 22 now, I managed to finish my course at university where all my friends claimed to have scored one or more times with girls, without me quite managing it. Since someone said my penis seemed rather small in the showers one day after a rugby match two years ago, it really seems to be shrinking. This shattered my confidence and I stopped getting firm erections even when I masturbated.

I felt so bad about this that I gave up athletics and football, and became what you call a computer nerd, preferring the Internet to basketball. Though I took some drugs in my teens, I think it was more a very bad attack of glandular fever I had when I was 15 that caused the trouble. Because I was very worried about this I went to see a psychiatrist who tried some tranquillizers on me which didn't seem to help at all and probably made the erection problem worse. Then I saw a urologist, who took one look at me and said it was a perfectly normal size and I should forget about it.

As I couldn't, I went to see an andrologist who took a careful history, examined me fully and did a detailed hormone profile. This showed a slight decrease in the free, active testosterone, perhaps due to the glandular fever or the stress of my final university exams, and he said that he would give me a short course of a mild form of testosterone called Proviron to boost my confidence.

That was six months ago, and it seemed to give me a kick start and make me feel confident enough to start a relationship with a girl, with whom I'm having regular sex. She really is very complimentary about my penis and it seems to respond very well to this, even though I've been off the Proviron for three months now.

Pellets

Pellets made of crystals of pure testosterone fused together under pressure or by heat have been made by the Belgian company Organon and used clinically since 1937. The safety and effectiveness of this preparation can be judged from the fact that it has been used virtually unchanged for nearly 60 years and has an excellent track record. Under a local anaesthetic, six to ten of the small cylindrical pellets, each containing 200 mg of testosterone, are introduced though a single large needle deep into the fat of the buttock. Apart from the initial sting of the local anaesthetic, it is a painless procedure taking about half an hour. It gives good levels of testosterone for around six months, and is still the longest acting and most steadily effective form of TRT available.[10] It also gives the most sustained and natural pattern of testosterone related hormones, with no excessive rise in DHT. The only occasional side-effect is that one or more of the pellets tracks to the surface and discharges itself, after which the puncture site heals over again.

Many patients enjoy the freedom from taking the testosterone undecanoate capsules on which they usually start and obtain very effective relief of andropausal symptoms from the pellet implant. One of the reasons why this is not a placebo reaction is not only that it goes on working for year after year, but that even when he does not know what to expect, the patient experiences a gradual return of symptoms every six months or so, which is obvious both to himself and his family. This is often reported as *'My battery is running down and I need a top up.'*

The long-term safety of correctly applied testosterone treatment in general, and this method in particular, has been clearly demonstrated by over 100 patients attending my clinic who have been kept free of andropausal symptoms by the implants for over five years now, especially three who have been treated for primary testicular failure since their teens with testosterone implants for 25, 35 and 50 years respectively. Ben, the latter, was one of the first patients in Britain to be treated by this method and his story is part of its history:

When I was a young boy, only 12 in fact, my father spotted that my testicles were not in the usual place, having stayed up in my abdomen. This was very worrying to me and my parents who thought I was never destined to go through puberty or become a proper man because I was suffering the then untreatable condition of what was called 'primary hypogonadism'.

Then at the age of 17, with no sign of a breaking voice or body hair like the other boys in my class at school, I had a lucky break by being referred to a Dr Peter Bishop, who was Professor of Endocrinology at Guy's Hospital in London. He had just been over to the USA and learned of a technique of implanting pellets of pure crystalline testosterone which they were using over there.

From 1944 onwards I started having the implants every six months into the side of my thighs, which was where they did them then. I got to know the clinic staff very well over the years, and they shared my pleasure in going through a normal, though somewhat late puberty, getting a job in the civil service, and then getting married at the age of 24. I had a happy, sexually active married life, but with no children, of course, as the undescended testicles never worked and had to be removed when I was 26 to prevent them developing cancer.

At the end of every six months, I could feel the effects of the testosterone beginning to wear off. At about the same time I started to feel tired, my interest in making love to my wife would die away and it became too much like hard work. The most severe of these withdrawal symptoms, though, were violent headaches, like bad migraine. Also my penis seemed to shrink in and my confidence just went. Within a fortnight of each implant I felt like a young lad again and generally more 'cock-sure' in every sense of the term. Girls looked nicer, my beard growth speeded up, my blood felt hotter and I seemed to glow with health.

Imagine my surprise and distress then when after being on the implants for over 47 years, I got a letter from the consultant who had taken over running the clinic to say that because of 'extreme cash pressures' they would no longer be providing an *implant service and we would have to go to our family doctors to get injections every two or three weeks. Sometimes when I'd missed an appointment at the clinic, I'd had to try these injections for a month or two and, like the couple of hundred other regulars at the clinic, I knew they were not nearly as good or as convenient and certainly didn't give anything like the same steady reliable benefits as the implants. It seemed a rather cynical move on some administrator's part to shift the expense of our testosterone treatment off the hospital budget onto that of family doctors round the country.*

Then I had my second lucky break and found a private doctor who was using the good old-fashioned pellet system. Everything is fine again now. I've been having the implants for another five years, taking me over the half century mark. This must say something about the safety of testosterone treatment as my six monthly blood checks show my body chemistry is fine, especially the prostate test, which is as low as that of a 30-year-old.

Though I've retired now, I feel very fit and have taken up growing moustaches of different styles, which I think make me look rather distinguished really. Certainly my wife must be very tickled by them, as we had sex five times last week, which is not bad for a nearly 70-year-old who got off to a slow start in this area of his life.

Patches

Different nationalities seem to have different favoured routes for taking medicines. The British persevere with their oral tradition and have a pill for every ill. The Americans are more impatient and direct, preferring injections, and have a shot for every spot. The French are a more sensuous race, favouring suppositories and creams; they find a pessary very necessary and that a balm can make you calm. So it was naturally a French doctor, Dr Jayle, who as long ago as 1942 prepared a cream containing testosterone and it became quite popular, with Frenchmen at least, who claimed it did wonders for their *amour propre*.[11] Frenchwomen were not so enamoured with this treatment because they found that the cream rubbed off onto them and while it enhanced desire, it put hair on their thighs and face, as reported by another French doctor, Dr Delanoe, in 1984.[12]

Undeterred, the French went on to develop a gel called Andractim, containing dihydrotestosterone (DHT), which they assured the ladies was quite safe because it was rapidly absorbed even when rubbed over a large area of manly chest twice a day. To make doubly sure, however, they recommended controlling passion for 10 minutes after application of the gel and then having a shower to wash off any excess. We must just hope that they read and obey the writing on the tube every time, because men usually need a large dose of testosterone to improve andropausal symptoms, while in women a little goes a long way! Also DHT alone, while promoting facial and body hair growth, as seen with mesterolone treatment, which trebles DHT levels, has generally less effect on libido or erection problems in most cases than the pellet implant, which leaves DHT levels unchanged.

The big breakthrough in patches came with the development by an American, Dr Virgil Place, working for the ALZA Corporation in Palo Alto, California. He developed a whole series of transdermal therapeutic systems (TTS), including the HRT patch for women, called Estraderm. As he told me once, he had 'a heck of a job' getting the female patch accepted. It was rather like the incredulity that Sir Walter Raleigh met with when he returned from America with a new drug delivery system consisting of the leaves of a plant which you dried, rolled up and then set fire to before you inhaled the smoke. However, like that system, once the HRT patch was marketed properly, it soon became a multi-million pound industry world-wide. Unlike smoking, though, it is a healthy habit giving benefit to millions of menopausal women.

As Dr Place explained, however, developing the male patch and getting it accepted gave even greater problems.[13] Firstly, a much larger dose of testosterone has to be delivered in the hormone deficient male than the minute amount of oestrogen needed in the menopausal female. Secondly, the only area of skin thin enough for the testosterone to get through was thought to be the scrotum, and there the skin was hairy and so sensitive that you couldn't use adhesives, which are irritant, to stick them on. So he came up with a patch called Testoderm, which was applied in the morning to the shaved scrotum, itself a ticklish business, and was renewed each day. This appliance of science became known as the 'Bals-Pratsch Patch', named after Dr Monika Bals-Pratsch of Munich University, who in 1986 was the first to report a clinically successful trial using the system.[14]

However, extensive trials of the system showed that it was inconvenient to use, likely to be expensive long term and had the theoretical disadvantage of producing an abnormal hormone profile. This was because the scrotal skin also happens to be the only area of the body rich in an enzyme called 5-alpha reductase, which converted the testosterone to DHT while it was being absorbed. For all these reasons, Testoderm was never marketed on a commercial basis and has now been superseded by a patch with an even more efficient delivery system which can be applied to any area of skin, even, like the female HRT patch, to the buttock.

Androderm, as the new patch is called, was developed by an American company called Theratech Inc., and is being marketed world-wide by SmithKline Beecham.[15] It is a very promising development and has undergone multi-centre controlled clinical trials showing its safety and efficacy in studies at Johns Hopkins University, the University of Utah and Karolinska Hospital in Stockholm, Sweden. It was found that two patches applied every night for periods of up to a year restored a normal hormonal pattern to nearly 100 'hypogonadal' men aged 15 to 65. The main side-effects were limited to slight skin irritation at the site of the patches, a common complication of the female HRT patch. With this excellent research data behind it, the patch received Federal Drug Administration marketing approval in America with a speed that surprised even the manufacturers and has just been released in the UK as Testopatch, causing renewed media interest in the whole subject of the andropause.

Here again controversy arises, because to meet with orthodox medical approval the manufacturers have obtained a licence to market the new patch for the treatment of male 'hypogonadism', which is an elastic-sided term meaning many different things to many different doctors. They might well take the view quoted in Lewis Carroll's *Through the Looking Glass*: *'"When I use a word," Humpty Dumpty said in a rather scornful tone, "it means just what I choose it to mean – neither more nor less."'*

The conventional medical definition of hypogonadism would be where the total plasma testosterone is below the 'normal range'. But we have seen, and the majority of andrologists would agree, that it is the free, biologically active testosterone, as represented by the FAI, which in actual fact determines the adequacy of testosterone for the body's needs. Strict application of the former definition, as my research has shown, would exclude over 85 per cent of patients with clear cut andropausal symptoms from the benefits of treatment with any testosterone preparation, including now the patch.

Also, there is no real agreement about what the so-called normal range actually is, particularly in men over the age of 40. Professor Alex Vermeulen in the University of Ghent in Belgium has spent a large part of his long and distinguished career in trying to establish this very point. He has found that studies to establish plasma levels of the male hormones at different ages can get totally different results according to whether you include or exclude either sick or exceptionally healthy men, particularly those over the age of 60. This does not include the effects on the levels of tissue testosterone and DHT, which are more than halved.[16] How do you establish a normal range to diagnose a condition, when 50, 60 or 70 per cent or more may be suffering some related symptoms which could be helped by treatment?

Add to that the variation of testosterone levels as measured in the same sample in different laboratories using a wide variety of methods, often giving different results, and the textbook definition of 'hypogonadism' loses most of its meaning in the real clinical world. The situation is made even worse by the fact that the units in which all the sex hormones are measured differ between America and Great Britain, together with the rest of Europe, two great nations divided by uncommon units, so that frequently doctors on one side of the Atlantic don't know what reference ranges the other side are using.

However, if the new patch can break through the

current terminology barrier limiting its use, it is likely to be a highly acceptable system. To some patients, who find other routes of treatment unattractive, it represents a breakthrough in treatment of the andropause. It will also be ideal for the type of double-blind controlled trials which are thought to be necessary to prove that drugs are effective in a particular condition.

Already some men are reporting being alarmed to find that they wake up in the morning with their partner's HRT patch sticking to them, it having rubbed off in the night and transferred itself. Fortu- nately, as the makers say, it's an unlikely accident, but how will the women feel when they wake up wearing a king-size male patch and have to get up and shave? Ah well, medicine is an imperfect science!

Results of TRT

The results of the study carried out on the first 400 of now over 1,000 of my andropausal patients in London gives, I think, good evidence that the andropause is a reality, due to either an absolute or relative deficiency of testosterone, which can be treated safely and effectively with TRT.

The age of the subjects ranged from 31 to 80, the mean being 54, which indicates the diverse range of often overlapping factors which can bring on the andropause. This gives it a wider age span than the traditional 45–55 which covers the onset of the menopause in women. Since the symptoms had on average been present for around four years, however, the peak time of onset is identical.

The mental symptoms included fatigue in 82 per cent, depression in 70 per cent and increased irritability in 60 per cent. The physical symptoms were aches, pains and stiffness, particularly in the hands and feet, in over 60 per cent, night sweats in 50 per cent and dryness and thinning of the skin in 46 per cent. Sexual problems were present in over 90 per cent, and included loss of libido and erectile problems both in around 80 per cent.

In addition to the changes associated with ageing, possible overlapping causes of these symptoms were stress in 60 per cent; alcohol in 35 per cent; a wide variety of medicines known to affect potency or which might lower testosterone in over 30 per cent; operations or injuries which might damage the testes or impair erection, especially in the 20 per cent with vasectomy, another 30 per cent; infections such as mumps, smoking and obesity all at around 20 per cent each.

Because of uncertainty about which form of testosterone might be most effective in relieving symptoms, and wishing to have a controlled comparison of the two treatment groups in this prospective study for research purposes, the patients were randomly allocated to medication with either mesterolone (MS) or testosterone undecanoate (TU). Both groups also received advice on general measures such as relaxation, drinking less, weight loss, exercise and wearing loose-fitting boxer shorts, and were followed up with the same range of detailed blood tests, andropausal symptom checklist and computerized psycho-social tests as in the initial 'work up' before treatment.

Depending on response and the patients' wishes, after six months of either of the oral treatments, testosterone pellet implantation (TI) was offered as a choice for long-term treatment.

Clinically, there was an overall feeling of increased vitality and well-being in all groups. Drive and assertiveness were observed to be increased by both the patients and their partners, but not to the point of aggression. In fact many became happier, less irritable and generally easier to live with, and felt they were coping better at work and in their family lives.

Increased hair growth, particularly on the chest and pubic region, was often noted by the patients. There was no hair loss from the scalp, and many felt the condition of their hair and skin had improved, with a markedly enhanced ability to tan. A few noted their hair colour had been restored. Penile enlargement and increased genital sensitivity were also noted with satisfaction by some.

Unpleasant side-effects were minimal, and limited to mild gastric irritation in a few patients on TU and the occasional loss of one or more pellets when the implants were rejected, which is an infrequent complication of this otherwise very convenient and effective form of treatment.

Andropausal symptom scores all fell statistically significantly and total sexual activity, which includes both intercourse and masturbation, increased in all three treatment groups. The benefits were most marked in the implant group, particularly in terms of increasing sexual activity and improving the relationship with the partner. Depression measures also decreased and went from being moderately severe back into the normal range.

On the safety side, blood pressures were unchanged or even fell slightly in the TU group after six months' treatment. There were no adverse changes in blood fat patterns, glucose, liver function tests or any part of the detailed blood profile. In particular, the early warning sign for prostate cancer, the prostate specific antigen (PSA), did not change at repeated tests up to five years, there were no signs of enlargement of the prostate clinically or on ultrasound scanning and no tumours developed.

Though a degree of placebo effect cannot be excluded in this type of study, it would not seem to account for either the magnitude or duration of the benefits, or the hormone changes in the expected direction which accompanied them. The very low test doses of either of the two oral testosterone derivatives given for the first month were effectively a form of placebo treatment. The subjects usually failed to respond to this, yet the placebo effect should then have been strongest. Only when the dose was doubled or trebled to therapeutic levels did they begin to feel the benefits.

Also with the implant treatment, it was only after two weeks, when the testosterone levels had risen, that the effects were experienced. Similarly, the observed benefits wore off and the symptoms, especially of fatigue, returned at around six months after the implant, when the hormone levels were dropping back towards their pre-treatment values.

Difficulties of Double-Blind Trials

George Bernard Shaw once remarked that doctors pour medicines, of which they know little, into patients, of whom they know less. In clinical practice today, the situation is probably much the same, but knowledge of the former is increasing, often at the expense of the latter.

Medicine has now become much more of a science than an art. What once seemed simple is now complex. Doctors used to give medicines and observe carefully what happened. If the patients seemed to improve, they continued to use the treatment and if they didn't, they stopped. Hormone treatments such as cortisone, thyroid hormone and insulin were introduced in this way because the benefits were blindingly obvious to doctors and patients alike, and could make the difference between life and death. In his use of testosterone in patients with severe arterial disease in the legs, Dr Jens Møller saw the dramatic benefits of treatment in preventing amputation for gangrene in the same light as giving insulin to diabetics and felt it would be unethical not to do so.

However, medical science, before it will accept any line of treatment as being proven, now demands what are known as 'double-blind control trials'. This means that the treatment on trial has to be given without either the patient or the doctor knowing whether active or placebo drug is being given at any one time. Depending on the design of the study, whether it is cross-sectional, longitudinal, cross-over or the exotic 'Latin-square', this can double, or even quadruple, the number of patients, the time needed and often the cost as well. It obviously limits the number of doctors who, without extensive and expensive research facilities, are able to undertake such studies, record and analyse them in the required statistical detail, and makes them more susceptible to commercial pressures in the design and interpretation of their studies.

Also, you now need to tell the patients that they are taking part in a trial and for them to give informed consent. This makes them dubious about the medicine and in private practice patients want to be sure that the specialist they see is not acting 'blindly', but giving them the best medicine for their particular case and that they are getting it straightaway. Where the medicine is effective in relieving their symptoms, in a double-blind trial the patients usually know before the doctor whether they are on the active drug or placebo. There is also the confounding effect of the other range of lifestyle modifications which the doctor will recommend in some patients and not in others and the variable placebo power of different doctors in encouraging the patients to undertake them.

The situation is even more difficult with testosterone treatment because, as was explained to me when I tried initially to get research funds, many of the preparations have been around for between 20 and 50 years, so that they are not only out of patent protection, but in the case of pellet implants, out of the product licence period. This limits the interest of drug companies in such products, unless there is a new and difficult to reproduce drug delivery system involved and they can see a large and guaranteed market.

Having said all this, some of the newer testosterone preparations such as the long-acting injections and patches may prove to be sufficiently 'sexy' for the drug companies or medical research organizations to subsidize scientifically 'pure' trials. In the meantime we will probably have to present the relatively 'impure' evidence of the practical experience of patients on treatment, combined with evidence from the literature and the type of cross-sectional research information on changes in symptoms and hormone levels reported in this chapter.

The data is there, carefully gathered over seven years in computerized format, testifying particularly to the safety and effectiveness of long-term testosterone treatment, and I cordially invite my medical colleagues from an academic medical background to examine, analyse and report on what I regard as a mine of interesting, important and exciting information.

Safety Factors

Concerns about the safety of the treatment naturally focus mainly on the prostate gland, the liver and the heart. In all these areas, except where methyl testosterone was used, long-term clinical experience in the 50 years in which a variety of testosterone treatments have been available, together with detailed reviews of the literature and the results of the serial investigations in this study, have been reassuring.

Some of the resistance to TRT which has arisen in the last two generations of physicians is undoubtedly due to the abuse of anabolic steroids by athletes and bodybuilders highlighted in a recent report. The occasional reports of mental and physical harm done by dangerous cocktails of these drugs being 'cycled' and 'stacked' in grossly excessive doses should not be allowed to detract from the excellent clinical experience over many years with carefully monitored therapeutic use. As the amounts taken by abusers are often 10 to 20 times the therapeutic doses, in men at least these illicit and thoroughly undesirable experiments appear to have proved most anabolic steroids have a considerable margin of safety.[17]

Also one could point to the use in multicentre WHO trials of high dose testosterone by injection as a male contraceptive. These injections in young healthy men to suppress sperm production give two or three times the natural hormone level which is the target for older men with severe andropausal symptoms, and so provide a resounding vote of safety for testosterone treatment.[18]

The debate on whether testosterone treatment might initiate cancer of the prostate is closely comparable to the controversy about whether female oestrogen replacement therapy would cause breast cancer. Just as most recent studies of HRT have shown little if any increase after up to 10 years' treatment with oestrogens, 50 years' treatment of hypogonadal patients with testosterone implants and 30 years of treatment with injections of testosterone enanthate do not show any rising incidence of prostate cancer of even benign hypertrophy.

Forty years ago studies were reported of 200 men over the age of 45, 100 of whom received intensive androgen therapy with no increase in the incidence of prostatic cancer or benign hyperplasia.[19] A recent review article on androgens and carcinoma of the prostate summarized the present informed view by stating: *'It is extremely unlikely that androgens play a role in the initiation of prostate cancer.'*[20]

Also, the area to be screened in the case of the prostate is the size of the thumb and ultrasound pictures give a very clear view of wherever cancer might arise. By contrast, the breasts are much more difficult to screen, X-rays which may themselves be harmful have to be used and there is no sensitive blood test like the PSA which can be used to exclude breast cancer.

A generation ago, women were arguing the same case in relation to whether treatment of their menopausal symptoms was flying in the face of nature. Fortunately, against stiff medical opposition, based largely on groundless worries over safety, they won that fight.[21] Moreover, as already noted, as the many benefits of long-term oestrogen treatment became apparent, largely through research work by clinician-based organizations such as the British Menopause Society, the interesting paradox arose that many alleged contraindications such as cardio-vascular disease, became positive indications.

In summary it can be concluded that HRT for men is

as safe, if not safer, than HRT for women. At least the men that have had the type of detailed 'well man' screen which is carried out prior to testosterone treatment know they are not harbouring prostate cancer, while many of their friends of the same age may be hosts to this silent assassin without knowing it until it is too late.

Future Directions in Testosterone Treatment

It seems certain that testosterone is a hormone whose time has finally come, and that TRT for men will take its rightful and very necessary place alongside HRT with oestrogen for women, as an integral part of preventive medicine in the twenty-first century. It is equally certain that new testosterone preparations will have to be introduced, as none of those presently available are ideal.

As an alternative to these treatments, it may be possible to stimulate the body's own natural production of testosterone, to slow its use and breakdown or lessen the factors antagonizing its action. It may also be feasible to liberate and activate the testosterone already produced by the body, which would give a form of testosterone-free testosterone treatment, an interesting therapeutic paradox.

Chapter Seven

Sexual Satisfaction

Sexual dissatisfaction was overall the commonest complaint of all in both my heterosexual and homosexual andropausal patients (92 per cent), as well as their partners (84 per cent). While in no way wishing to suggest that sex is the be all and end all of a marriage or other long-term partnership, as one patient put it, 'It is more than just the icing on the cake – it is one of the most important and binding of the basic ingredients.' Even the Catholic Church recognizes non-consummation as one of the few grounds for nullifying a marriage and there is an old saying that the rocks on which a marriage breaks up are usually to be found in the bed. So what can you do when, as the perennially active rock star of the Rolling Stones, Mick Jagger, sings, you *'can't get no satisfaction'*?

Is It your Age?

Though most people assume that sexual activity is likely to decrease with age, in the swinging sixties, the experts gave a rather different picture. They, together with more recent investigators, found that sexual interest and morning erections, a good marker for either actual or potential erectile power, declined very gradually with age and only went below the 50 per cent mark in the nineties. The actual frequency of sexual intercourse dropped away much more rapidly, however, and reached the 50 per cent mark at around 70, mainly due to erectile failure.[1]

Shakespeare recognized this problem 400 years ago when he wrote, *'Is it not strange that desire should so many years outlive performance?'* This question taxes the minds of doctors and their patients to this day. The answer could well be that lower levels of testosterone are needed to maintain libido than are required for potency. There are also many complex circulatory factors involved in obtaining an erection as well as in the hormonal drive. The spirit is still willing often long after the flesh has weakened, though following repeated erectile failure, the desire tends eventually to fade also. It is difficult to assess what is essentially physical and what psychological, a combination of expectations, attitude and monogamy leading to monotony.

The spirit is often still willing, though, long after the flesh has weakened. This is likely to become even more of a problem as more and more women go on long-term HRT at the menopause. In such cases the big drop in sexual interest and enjoyment which was well documented for women in their fifties has declined or even been reversed. Yet this is just the time when andropausal men are experiencing the biggest decline in both libido and potency. So women's expectations of continuing sexual activity are rising year by year and men are literally not able to keep up with them. Increasingly, couples are likely to get sexually out of step, particularly as men tend to marry women a few years younger than themselves, with the male left lagging further and further behind.

A loving sexual relationship is not only enjoyable, though, but can actually keep you young. Evidence from a recent study by a Dr David Weeks, a clinical neuropsychologist at the Edinburgh Royal Infirmary, suggests that the ageing process can be delayed by making love more than twice a week. He recruited a group of people in Europe and America who claimed to look and feel much younger than they actually were and got them to send him their photos and fill in a lifestyle questionnaire. He also asked a control group from the same part of each country to do the same and then got independent assessors to guess the age of all 3,500 people, who ranged in age from their twenties to over 100.

The results were clear cut, the youthful test group being rated as 12 to 14 years on average younger than they actually were and the control group one or two years younger. The differences on the questionnaire were even more striking, the 'young lovers' having sex much more often than their peers, and many, both men and women, having much younger partners. However, an important feature of any relationship was that it was a loving and happy one.

This is similar to the results on factors which prevent coronary heart disease. A group in the Netherlands showed that feeling loved was one of the most important things that kept heart trouble away. As Woody Allen says, *'Love is the answer, but sex raises some interesting questions.'* Perhaps if we can answer some of these questions, the loving element will have a greater chance to express itself.

Sexual Chemistry

Testosterone is the hormone which largely regulates desire in both men and women, although its levels are generally 10 to 20 times higher in the male. It is thought to act both directly on the brain, and indirectly in making the genital areas more sensitive and responsive, also enlarging the penis or clitoris. Thus it is generally a sexual stimulant for both sexes.

Experience with patients and research reviewed by Professor Bancroft of the Medical Research Council Reproductive Biology Unit in Edinburgh in his book *Human Sexuality and its Problems* suggest that there is less overlap between the laboratory 'normal range' of testosterone and its 'behaviourally relevant range' in men than in women.[2] This means that if the laboratory measures testosterone levels in 100 'normal' men, age and sexual activity often unspecified, in 95 per cent values of say 10–30 nmol/l may be recorded. Many studies, including my own, have shown that the libido will be increased by testosterone treatment in men whose values lie in the range 5–15 nmol/l, though the proportion of free, biologically active, hormone is, as emphasized elsewhere, also very important.

However, in women, the 'normal range' is only 1–2 nmol/l, but libido may go on rising up to 7–10 nmol/l or even higher. This is shown by testosterone treatment, both orally and by pellet implant, for those suffering lack of desire or who lose their ability to have an orgasm for no obvious psychological reason. It is also reported in women self-medicating with very high doses of testosterone, either in athletes or those wishing to become 'The Third Sex' *(see page 53)*.

That the level of free, biologically active testosterone is vital to libido in both sexes and sexual function in

the male is shown by studies on epileptics. Anti-epileptic drugs raise the sex hormone binding globulin protein, holding the testosterone in the blood and preventing
it acting.[3] Both the libido and morning erections are reduced while patients take these drugs, but when they come off them, the binding protein levels fall, their testosterone is freed up again and the libido and morning erections are restored.[4] This is a perfect model of the male menopause and conclusively demonstrates its reversibility.

The Science of Sexual Attraction

Poets and songwriters have mused for millennia why it is that people fall in love. Psychologists and pharmacologists may now have cracked the problem between them. Though their results may not immediately improve their love life or ours, they offer hope for an understanding.

The psychologists have discovered the effects of early imprinting and bonding which occur at birth and in infancy. The newborn child is not the passive plastic doll it was once thought to be, but a highly receptive, rapidly developing, sentient being. It is aware of, responds to and learns from the complex inputs from all its faculties. Even in the subdued pink gloom of the womb it is thought to be soothed by the rhythmic beating of the mother's heart, the whooshing of the blood flowing in her abdominal vessels and the inner reverberations of her voice.

At birth, it is catapulted into the blinding light of a chilly operating theatre, held upside-down and slapped until it cries as its mother screams with the pain of childbirth. In the best of natural childbirth practices, though hi-tech help is at hand if needed, the child is immediately reunited with its mother, held lovingly in her arms, gazes through the accurately fixed focus of its eyes at her face, and listens to her soft and gentle voice. In the first few minutes and hours afterwards, like all mammals, there is a complex emotional and physical bonding process involving all the senses, which will last for life. If this goes well, it can lay firm foundations for emotional stability throughout childhood and adult life. If it is disrupted by separation, illness or emotional or physical trauma to mother or child, it can leave lasting psychological damage.

It is probable that the variations and mishaps which occur in this bonding process leave the corresponding small or large psychological scars which decide whether and how we are going to bond from puberty onwards. After all, dogs separated from their mothers in the first few hours or days of life and weaned by humans, often seem to assume they are human and relate more to human beings than they do to other dogs. The biologist Konrad Lorenz first reported how geese he held immediately after hatching and fed for the first few days of life became imprinted on him and for the rest of their lives waddled after him, convinced they were eminent biologists. Cygnets similarly reared by a cameraman would follow him anywhere, whether he was walking, in a car or in a boat. As fully grown birds they could then be trained to carry light cameras on their backs and achieve beautiful films of formations of swans in flight from literally a bird's eye view.

With models like this, is it any wonder that men tend to fall in love with women who resemble their mothers, either in their looks, the tone of their voices or possibly even the way they smell?

Pheromones

Even more than by sight and sound, throughout the animal kingdom, Cupid's arrows are carried by bodily scents. Dogs seeking out the bitch on heat, the musk ox that can scent a potential mate miles away and the stallion that catches the scent of the mare are timeless examples. Though perfumes were developed thousands of years ago mainly to cover up unpleasant body odours with more attractive ones, the more skilled perfumiers learned from the ability of animals to smell and be sexually attracted by the opposite sex before they catch sight of them.

The term 'pheromone' was coined by the German biochemist Adolf Butenandt in 1959 and was another of his major contributions to science, the first being his discovery and synthesis of testosterone nearly 25 years previously (*see page 21*). The term is derived from the Greek *phero* ('to carry') and *hormao* ('to excite'). This is an apt description of these airborne chemical messages promising sexual excitement, a sort of long-range biological dating agency.

Though first described in female silkworm moths, pheromones were also found in female monkeys and in women, where they peaked at the time of ovulation and were under the control of oestrogen. Thus it was shown that from the time when oestrogens surged at puberty, the inner female hormones started the production of these outer chemical signs of sexual maturity and availability.

The main sex hormone in men, the androgen testosterone, acts similarly. It is broken down into two components called androstenone and androstenol, which at a subliminal level are thought to be powerful sexual attractants. They are released in the odours of the armpits and scrotum, in urine and in saliva. Andro-stenone gives a characteristic smell to male urine and is what the sow is detecting when snuffling for truffles, which is perhaps why this rare and exotic fungus has a reputation for being an aphrodisiac. Androstenol has a musky odour, which is less obvious, but probably equally potent.

As the average female nose is at the height of the average male armpit, dancing can be seen as an intense form of exchange of bodily scents preceding the exchange of bodily fluids.

After the andropause, because of the low testosterone levels, the phermonally deprived male does not feel as sexy or smell as sexy as the pungent, sexually active man in his prime. Research urgently needs to be done to see whether pheromones are restored by hormone replacement therapy with the parent compound, testosterone.

Ready for Love

Why is it that in spring a young man's fancy lightly turns to thoughts of love? Well, even though the mating season isn't what it used to be, probably because of all the year round stimulation by artificial lighting and tele-vision, there are good reasons for this in terms of the hormonal rites of spring.

As the urban cave dweller emerges blinking into the spring sunshine, he drinks up the sun. This is seen particularly in the more northern countries such as Scandinavia, where the winter nights are long and the days often overcast with clouds. There people often just sit out in the open sunning themselves as though mentally thawing out.

As already explained, the bright light and lengthening

days have the effect of reducing the level of melatonin, the 'hibernation hormone'. Some people seem to get a surge of this hormone in the autumn and it makes them feel quite torpid and depressed, a condition known as seasonal affective disorder, or SAD for short. This can be prevented or treated by midwinter sunshine holidays or by bursts of intense artificial daylight.

In spring, the reduction in the production of melatonin not only causes generally greater mental alertness, but also raises levels of a variety of brain chemicals, called neurotransmitters, which stimulate and arouse us, making us full of the joys of spring.

Because these neurotransmitters regulate mood, they have been the target for intensive study by most of the major pharmaceutical companies, who see the potential market for the chemical production of happiness, peace and love in bottled form. Aldous Huxley in his book *Brave New World* back in the 1920s first coined the advertising slogan for the mythical drug 'Soma' of *'Take a gram and don't give a damn.'* Unfortunately since then there have been many false dawns. The prototypic tranquillizer Valium was originally marketed with pictures of tigers changed into pussy-cats. In the same way, some of the early anti-depressant drugs showed pictures of space rockets lifting off for the moon to illustrate the hoped-for lifting of the spirits. However, though they have proved useful in some cases of severe depression, the results have often been somewhat depressing to patients and doctors alike. Unfortunately it has been found that if you take the edge off the 'razor-blade of life down which we slide', according to the American humorist Tom Lehrer, you take the edge off many of life's joys also and blunt performance and creativity.

So it seems that the complex mysteries of the human brain still elude our grasp. Though advances in psychopharmacology are steadily improving the drugs available for mental ailments, we cannot safely manipulate mood without risking severe side-effects. We have been able to get to the Sea of Tranquillity on the moon, but still come back to a sea of tranquillizers on the Earth.

Unfortunately, it is in the field of sexual activity that the undesirable side-effects of tranquillizers, anti-depressants and sleeping pills are most severe and unpleasant. For liveliness, loving, libido and the pursuit of sexual fulfilment, we need just the right mixture of hormones and neurotransmitters, in the right brain cells, at the right time. Drug treatments are at present very hit and miss. This is why unless anxiety and/or depression are very severe and prolonged it is generally better to use gentle non-drug approaches such as psychotherapy and psychosexual counselling – meditation rather than medication.

The Food of Love

There are some foods which may gently enhance both desire and sexual activity, through regulating brain chemistry.

Two of the most important neurotransmitters in the brain are serotonin and the mono-amines. Serotonin is derived from a plasma amino acid called tryptophan and after this is taken up into the brain, a good supply of vitamin B_6 is needed for its conversion. Most diets contain sufficient protein to supply the necessary trypto-phan and too much protein may increase competition from other amino acids for uptake into the brain. These competing amino acids can be removed by the release of insulin, so simple sugars such as glucose and sucrose, which produce this, will improve the uptake of tryptophan and hence the production of serotonin.

The predominant brain mono-amine is noradrena-line. It is produced in the brain, again with the help of vitamin B6, from the amino-acid tyrosine. This is also present in most proteins and is easily taken up into the brain in proportion to the amount of protein in the diet.

Another mono-amine is phenylethylamine, which is present in chocolate and may account for its reputed aphrodisiac properties.

Armed with all this essential biochemical informa-tion, we can concoct a meal almost guaranteed to stimu-late passion. After the relaxing champagne, which also stimulates female testosterone production, we have the suggestive goat's cheese starter, redolent with mono-amines. This is followed by the minute steak, to boost tyrosine, new potatoes with butter, again to help testos-terone production, and a fresh green salad to enhance vitamin C levels. The *coup de grâce* is the 'death by choco-late' cake, topped with B6-rich walnuts. This is surely a recipe for sexual success, providing it doesn't bring on a splitting migraine headache in the woman or an instant heart attack in the man.

Can Sexual Satisfaction Be Improved?

Certainly it is possible in the vast majority of andropausal cases to improve sexual satisfaction for both partners, not only by TRT, but also by a range of additional techniques such as sex education, focusing particularly on the physical, hormonal and emotional changes occurring in the male, and, where necessary, psychosexual counselling or couples therapy. With reas-surance that there may be a physical basis for the male partner's apparent lack of desire, as well as his unwill-ingness or inability to perform, a tense situation can often be defused and the relationship helped on the road to recovery.

In particular, emphasizing the good non-sexual areas of the relationship and the enjoyment that both partners get from them can reduce the friction. One or both may also need to learn a good relaxation technique, as described in the next chapter, and small amounts of alcohol, such as a shared bottle of wine, can help.

For most couples, when the first flush of passion is over, a sexual session needs time and energy. Erections are more difficult for a man to maintain when he is rushed or tired or both. If one or both partners are under pressure, a 'dating' system may help when they chose a time and place they feel most relaxed and happiest together. One patient, when I suggested this, said he and his wife had such different conflicting time deadlines in their busy lives that it was rather like timing a moon shot. If it works, however, by some mysterious process it usually gets easier and easier to find time for these love-making sessions.

Massage, especially in subdued light or candlelight, and with music to soothe the savage breast, can be both relaxing and a turn on, as well as being part of 'getting in touch'. Kind, loving, encouraging comments on the other person and the effect they are having on you work much better than even the most constructive criticism. Fortunately, nature is kind in that we tend to get long-sighted around the age of 50, so that skin blemishes and the occasional wrinkle are blurred over, and hopefully we remember how we wanted our partners to look, or they did look, in their physical prime.

Such methods are all part of encouraging the realization that sexual activity can be pleasant and satisfying even without penetration. Usually under sufficiently relaxed conditions both partners can have orgasms by mutual masturbation, oral sex or any of the increasing variety of 'sex-aids' that can be bought mail-order or from a local store. Sexy garments, perhaps chosen by the other person, also have their part to play in setting the scene.

Fortunately, with the more frank approach that medical assessment and treatment encourages, combined with these common sense self-help measures, the situation usually improves to the point where full intercourse resumes or becomes more satisfying. If this doesn't happen and there still appears to be a large anxiety or emotional part to the problem, then a more gradual approach under the guidance of a properly qualified sex-therapist should be tried. The therapist will often advise a technique known as 'sensate focus', which involves stages of being touched for your own pleasure without genital contact, then giving feedback on what you find enjoyable as well as unpleasant, and finally enjoying the experience of touching and being touched, including genital contact and, if it happens, orgasm, though this is not the aim.

Premature ejaculation, which often accompanies erectile difficulties, can be treated by medication, as described later, or by a 'stop-start' technique, initially by hand, and then with the woman sitting astride the man to give better control of withdrawal and re-entry.[5] Alternatively, the 'squeeze' method described originally by Masters and Johnson in 1970,[6] can be used. Here, when the man is about to ejaculate, the woman gently but firmly squeezes the base of the head of the penis until the impulse to ejaculate subsides.

One worrying statistic is that in a community-based study in the United States, of the sample men, aged between 40 and 70, just over half felt that their erections were inadequate. This is also the commonest presenting problem in male sexual dysfunction clinics and peaks at the time when the andropause appears, that is the mid-forties onwards.[7] This is a major health problem which is seldom adequately investigated or treated. So at this stage it is appropriate to describe how erections happen so that we can better understand what can go wrong, especially with age or an insufficient hormonal head of steam, and how to help.

The Mechanics of Erection

You will remember Mae West's famous remark to an enthusiastic cowboy who came to her saloon, *'Is that a gun in your pocket, or are you just glad to see me?'*

Man's ability to have an erection, which has been worshipped from the earliest of times, is actually a recurring miracle of hydraulic engineering. It is brought about by a complex series of chemical changes and nerve reflexes, which work together to increase the amount of blood flowing into the penis and temporarily decrease the amount going out. Two elongated blood sacks, the *corpora cavernosa*, become engorged and create the erection. This event, which is achieved with effortless and sometimes embarrassing ease in the teens and twenties, usually becomes a more difficult feat in the thirties and forties, can be variable in the fifties and sixties, and is often a disappointingly brief and infrequent wonder in the seventies and beyond, especially in the 'hormonally challenged' andropausal male.

For the amount of blood going into the penis to be adequate for an erection, there needs to be a good flow of blood in the artery to the penis, relaxation of the blood vessels inside it and reduction of the amount of blood draining out. It is rather like pumping up a bicycle tyre and hoping for a smooth ride. It you don't pump hard enough, if the walls of the inner tube are perished or stuck together, or if the valve is leaky and lets the air out as fast as it goes in, only hopes are inflated.

Sometimes the small artery supplying blood to the penis is clogged up because of a generalized arterial degeneration called atheromatosis, which is the most common cause of coronary heart disease. This is more frequent in those with high blood cholesterol levels, in diabetics and in smokers, who are more prone to erection problems. Fortunately, it is seldom sufficient on its own to cause the problem, and when it is, arterial surgery to provide additional blood supply is occasionally successful.

The pooling of blood in the penis which produces its rigidity is dependent on hormonal priming, local chemical factors and a balance of nerve stimulation. Because of the complexity of this mechanism, it is easily upset by hormonal insufficiency, a wide range of medications and emotional reactions, especially anxiety. Each of these needs to be considered in cases of erectile difficulty and corrected where possible. Often the patient and his partners efforts to overcome the problem are just as important as the doctor's.

The story seems appropriate here of the man who went to seek medical advice and was given treatment which needed a lot of lifestyle changes and self-effort. Being by nature a lazy fellow, before he left the consulting-room he disbelievingly asked the white-coated man sitting behind the desk, *'Are you a real doctor?'*

'The question is,' said the doctor, *'are you a real patient?'*

Testosterone and Erectile Function

Though it is difficult to say precisely what part testosterone plays in helping to produce erections, it certainly both primes the penis and triggers the chain of events which bring an erection about. It is surprising but gratifying how often when adequate testosterone therapy is given, all the symptoms of the andropause disappear within a few weeks or months, including erectile difficulties, particularly when other factors contributing to its onset or continuation are dealt with. A statistically highly significant improvement in erectile function occurred in over 70 per cent of my first 400 cases treated with a variety of different forms of testosterone. This was particularly marked with the more powerful oral preparation, Restandol, which sometimes needed to be given in high but safe doses, and with the pellet implants.

Though this use of testosterone to help erection problems is controversial and not acknowledged by some authorities, which say it only increases frustration without giving back the means to perform, this is certainly not my experience in this large group of patients. The efficiency of testosterone in restoring potency is a common experience with doctors prepared to give it an adequate trial. It was even recognized over 50 years ago in the article on the 'male climacteric' by Drs Heller and Myers described in detail in the first chapter of this book (*see pages 23–7*). They found that erectile function returned in nearly all of their testosterone deficient patients when they gave the hormone and went away again when they stopped.[8]

Even though it is more difficult to restore function than desire, unless the source of the problems is obviously psychological, it seems logical to investigate the level of free active testosterone and boost it if it is low. If nothing else, the accompanying increases in libido, confidence and energy will greatly encourage the patient to try supplementary mechanical and medicinal methods, if needed.

Sexercise

Sex is the most vigorous form of exercise most people take and for some it is the only form. Measurements of pulse rate, blood pressure and hormones before, during and afterwards have shown surges in the stress hormones during sexual activity, together with rises in heart rate and blood pressure. Fortunately, these go down to baseline levels or even below in the recovery phase afterwards and there is then an increase in testosterone in both sexes.

For this reason, regular sexual activity, even if the man cannot always achieve penetration, is to be encouraged in the prevention and treatment of the andro- pause. If this is not possible, either because a partner is not available or not willing, then masturbation about once a week stops the erectile system 'going rusty', and may stimulate testosterone production. As Woody Allen says, *'At least masturbation is sex with someone you love.'* From the medical point of view occasional masturbation can be beneficial, as long as it doesn't get out of hand.

Drugs which Help and Drugs which Hinder

Drugs given for medical reasons can often play a part in bringing on the erectile problems which contribute to the menopause. The motto is 'If in doubt, check it out.'

Virtually any drug used to reduce the blood pressure,

but especially diuretics and the so-called beta-blockers, can be a problem here.⁹ Because hypertension is often stress related and not so much an illness as a way of life, stress management techniques can be tried to control mild to moderate elevations in blood pressure *(see pages 204–8)*. Reduced stress will also help to reduce the performance anxiety element in erection problems.

Alternatively, sometimes switching to a different preparation, such as Labetolol (Tranxene) or the new 'alpha-blockers', which seem to interfere less with erections, can be helpful in combination with testosterone treatment. TRT does not itself generally raise blood pressure and may in some cases lower it.

A wide variety of tranquillizers and anti-depressants are also associated with impaired erections. These are used to treat many conditions with symptoms which overlap with those of the menopause, so it is often not clear which is doing what.¹⁰ Virtually all anti-depressants can have a harmful effect, except possibly the newer generation of drugs such as Prozac. Prozac is occasionally helpful in treating depression associated with the andropause and it also seems to reduce the common tendency to premature ejaculation which accompanies difficulty in maintaining an erection.

The newer compounds have a different action on the brain from those used to treat depression, by inhibiting the uptake of a chemical by which one brain cell activates another, 5 hydroxy-tryptamine (5HT). Some specialists are sufficiently enthusiastic about this type of compound to recommend its use in premature ejaculation, though through limited experience this may prove to be a case of premature ejudication. A new anti-depressant called Venlafaxine (Efexor) made by Wyeth is reputed to have the least effect on libido or erectile function and few side-effects generally.

Another possible exception is the older anti-depressant, Trasadone, marketed in the UK as Molypaxin. Given as a single dose of 75 to 150 mg half an hour before sex, it can in some cases help in obtaining erections over a one to two hour period. Its effectiveness varies widely from person to person and it may just make them feel sleepy, which is not usually the desired effect.

Asthma treatments such as ephedrine and many other inhalers can also sometimes make erection problems worse, and a trial of withdrawing or switching treatment where possible can help.

Even stomach medicines such as Tagamet have infrequently been shown to cause problems, as have a seemingly endless list of medicines.[11]

Drugs of addiction appear only to be a problem if being used in large amounts and causing psychological or social problems. They may, however, accompany an alcohol problem, or be used to avoid facing up to the issues contributing to the andropause. The appropriate agencies such as Narcotics Anonymous may need to be involved here. The commonest drug of addiction, nicotine, can also be a threat to potency and for this and many other health reasons is best avoided. It has been found that one cigarette can reduce penile blood flow by one third. Though smoking once had a sexy image, we now understand why macho film stars are only seen smoking *after* sex scenes, or else a long time before.

Though erection problems often decrease or even disappear with combined treatment with testosterone and the other measures described, there may be some continuing difficulty, particularly in diabetics or those with heart and circulatory problems. In such cases, there are a range of other measures which can usually solve the problem one way or another.

Yohimbine, marketed in Britain and the USA as Yocon, is a preparation of the bark of an African tree, *Pausinystalia yohimbe*, which when taken by mouth in some cases seems to act on the brain as a sexual stimulant, both boosting the libido and improving erections, particularly in people on testosterone. It is usually taken as one 5.4 mg tablet three times a day, or alternatively as between one and three tablets half to one hour before intercourse, which I have found a more effective and economic method. Yohimbine shouldn't be given to nervous individuals, who can become more anxious on it, or those with high blood pressure, where it can have an unpredictable effect.

There are also a variety of substances which can be injected into the penis by the patient himself just before intercourse to provide a serviceable and sustained erection. Many urologists encourage the patient to go straight for this option, without detailed examination for signs and symptoms of the andropause. This is a pity, as many men find it a bit cold-blooded and premeditated, and their partners find it unromantic, mechanical and sometimes an insult to their sex appeal. As one wife said, inaccurately in her husband's case, '*If I were as attractive as Marilyn Monroe, he would get an erection immediately, wouldn't he?*' So, though this treatment has a high success rate, with usually around two thirds of even resistant cases responding, about half the people who say they'll try it drop out because they or their partners find it unacceptable.

Papaverine is the most commonly used of these injections, and is a cheap and stable preparation. It is injected through a short and very fine needle into the shaft of the penis, and increases the flow of blood into the two spongy *corpora cavernosa*, helping to produce and maintain an erection. According to the carefully regulated amount injected from the small syringe provided, which is similar to that used by diabetics, the length of time the erection is maintained can be adjusted, according to taste and joint enthusiasm of the partners, from a quarter of an hour to one hour or more. Moreover, it carries on even after the man has reached orgasm and ejaculated, which some couples find adds to their enjoyment.

Apart from its artificiality, there are other drawbacks to this treatment, however. The slight stinging pain experienced when the needle is jabbed into this very sensitive part of the male anatomy and the possibility of bruising, especially if the patient is on anticoagulants or even aspirin, can be off-putting. Also, sometimes erections persist for several hours or more, which can be dangerous as well as uncomfortable and socially inconvenient. If an erection lasts for more than four hours, it is known medically as priapism. This should be dealt with as soon as possible in a hospital casualty department to avoid bruising which may last days if not weeks.

More gentle in its action and less liable to cause priapism is the injection of alprostadil, a preparation similar to the natural substance in the body called prostaglandin E1. This has recently been introduced in this country by, appropriately, Upjohn Pharmaceuticals, as Caverject. This is a definite advance, but tends to cost about the same as a bottle of champagne for each shot, and even if you can afford the expense, unlike champagne, it is not recommended for use more than three times a week.

There are rumours, however, of a real breakthrough being tested in Israel, in the form of a prostaglandin cream which can be absorbed through the skin. There is also a tiny pellet of alprostodil, which can be inserted into the opening of the urethra at the tip of the penis, and is rapidly absorbed into the *corpora cavernosa*. The system known as MUSE (Medicated Urethral System for Erection) is made by VIVUS in the USA, and marketed by Astra in Europe. These preparations will hopefully have the same effect as the injections, but be less painful, less expensive and much more acceptable to both partners.

Mechanical Methods

There are a variety of mechanical devices which can be used to promote the flow of blood into the penis and lessen the amount going out. The simplest of these is a rubber ring, usually called the Blako ring, which comes in different sizes and, when rolled down the semi-erect penis, reduces the outflow of blood in the veins, which can help to obtain and maintain a full erection.

Another aid is a suction device consisting of a glass tube which is slipped over the penis and applies negative pressure gently to it by means of a mechanical pump (Erectoid). When a full erection has been achieved, a tight elastic band similar to the Blako ring is slipped off the end of the tube nearest the patient and prevents the blood in the penis from flowing away. However, many men find this way of getting an erection cumbersome, unromantic and even painful, so it leaves a lot to be desired.

Surgical Techniques

Rarely, none of these treatments work and then the opinion of a urologist specializing in this field should be sought. After investigation of the arterial inflow and venous outflow of the penis, they may recommend vascular surgery, or one of the inflatable or soft metal, 'bendy-toy' penile implants. All these methods can produce good results in the right hands, but none of them are much use if the other symptoms of the menopause, especially lack of libido, are untreated.

Good Times Coming

Finally, there is good news long term. Within three to five years erection problems may largely be a thing of the past.

There have been very promising new developments recently in the field of nitric oxide and the erectile mechanism. A new type of nerve has recently been discovered in many organs in the body, including the penis, which, amongst other important actions, relaxes the smooth muscle fibres controlling the diameter of small blood vessels. These are known as 'nitrurgic' nerves because by releasing nitric oxide they allow the blood vessels in the penis to dilate and then become engorged with blood, producing an erection.

Anything which helps nitric oxide production or activity encourages the erection. Amyl nitrate has been used for sexual stimulation, as well as its ability to relax smooth muscle in various parts of the body.

Pharmacologists have, as you can imagine, been working round the clock to synthesize a drug which would prolong the action of nitric oxide. One topical application, in both senses of the word, is a cream which, when applied to the shaft of the penis half an hour before intercourse, is absorbed through the skin, causing engorgement of the *corpora cavernosa*, so that erection is greatly helped. A very well-conducted and encouraging trial of this pharmacological cocktail was recently reported in the *British Medical Journal* article by an Egyptian Professor, Adel Gomaa[12].

The principles used in preparing this cream *Taminox*, which works on several different erectile mechanisms at once, including nitric oxide, have been taken further and combined with the priming action of testosterone in Britain, where we are carrying out trials at this time.

As far as oral preparations go, at present the drug company Pfizer appears to be ahead of the field. They have come up with a drug taken by mouth which helps nitric oxide to work, so that its active agents accumulate in the walls of the penile blood vessels, keeping them relaxed and the penis erect. This eagerly awaited preparation is called Viagra, also known as sildenafil, and one tablet taken an hour before intercourse brings on a sustained erection lasting for up to three hours in 90 per cent of cases. It is currently undergoing its last clinical trials, and should be on the market before the end of the century – truly a giant leap for mankind.

Chapter Eight

Secrets of Vitality and Virility

What conclusions can be drawn from these ideas about factors affecting men's health at different times of life? I believe there are lessons for society, as well as individuals living in that society, and what affects the well-being of one will affect the well-being of the other. Pollution of the external environment with xeno-oestrogens for example, can have life-long effects on the male, from causing the birth of a child with impaired sexuality to creating a subfertile male more prone to having a severe mid-life crisis and premature andropause. Probably the best way of drawing these strands together is to consider the causes of the andropause and the possibilities for avoiding and treating this drop in both vitality and virility, one by one.

The Male Psyche under Threat

The fight for masculinity is a life-long battle, with both chemical and psychological warfare involved.

First, early prevention in terms of producing a male infant best equipped to maintain his masculinity for life must be undertaken, by first identifying the sources of xeno-oestrogens in the environment and then reducing them. The 'battle of the sexes' could also be called the 'battle of the hormones', because generally male and female hormones have opposite and opposing actions, and currently, men are losing the fight, as seen in the falling sperm count.

Many of the battlegrounds are social and psychological, so these also need to be considered when planning for the future health of men. This struggle is evident in everything from clothing to work. For example, as well as reducing fertility and testosterone levels by raising the temperature of the testes, jeans are also symbolic of the identity and role crisis in the adolescent male. If everyone is wearing the trousers, mentally as well as physically, what's so special about being male?

Also, there is a trend for women to be more sexually assertive, both in the East and West. In Japan, a few of what used to be shy retiring office girls are flaunting their sexuality, dancing provocatively in the scantiest of costumes during *bodycon* (body consciousness) evenings, stuffing banknotes into the posing pouches of hunky male strippers and choosing a string of lovers. In the West, the feminists, having got most people thoroughly confused about what is really expected of the 'New Man' are tending to turn on each other, and there is a fashion to alternate between heterosexual and homosexual relationships. There are groups for women who want to experience dressing, walking and talking like a man. Meanwhile, some young girls are tasting the delights of gang warfare and forming bands of highly aggressive muggers who occasionally become killers.

Increasing numbers of men who used to bond with body contact activities such as the rugby scrum are now holding hands and exploring the feminine side of themselves in encounter groups.

Many men stagger away from the divorce courts with little more than the clothes they stand up in, while alimony, palimony and child support lessen their financial independence. Loss of work from factors such as computerization and the world-wide recession can also at any time cast them in the unaccustomed role of 'house-husband'. This can make them feel redundant both socially and sexually. In the intellectually prestigious Oxford Union, women debate the motion 'A woman needs a man like a fish needs a bicycle.'

In my practice I am seeing increasing numbers of young men in their teens and twenties with what could be called the 'locker-room syndrome'. This is an anxiety state where they do not feel sufficiently masculine in terms of their physique, body hair or penile proportions. In its fully developed state it can cause agonizing self-doubt to the extent of avoiding sexual relationships altogether, stopping playing team sports which might involve communal bathing afterwards and in extreme cases even avoiding public urinals where unfavourable comparisons might be made.

This is made worse by the increasing sexual experience of women. They may have had several better endowed lovers in the past, or have seen hard or soft-porn videos or magazines. These, as the young men are painfully aware, always feature handsome, muscular males well equipped to have sex non-stop, *'bonking like beam engines for hours on end'* to use the words of a woman TV interviewer. As one Indian Army officer said after watching a mammoth performance by an elephant servicing a female, *'That's a tough act to follow.'*

This is a difficult condition to treat and endless reassurance along the lines of *'It's not the size that counts'*

doesn't seem to help. General psycho-sexual counselling, sometimes over several months, together with
assertiveness training, and hopefully a loving supportive
relationship with a partner, gives the best hopes of a
cure. Sometimes a brief course of testosterone in low
doses can produce more assertiveness, boost confidence
and induce a more macho mood in which the penis feels
more adequate and erections are stronger. Penile exten-
sion operations, even in men who are in stable relationships and have fathered children, are beginning to be
performed on National Health Service patients in Britain
and in private plastic surgery clinics throughout the
world. However, an operation may well not be successful and this seems an expensive physical approach to
what is essentially a psychological problem.

There are other factors also which are making
women, particularly in mid-life, sometimes feel sexier
and act more assertively than their male counterparts.
Just as increasing numbers of men are fading fast due
to an unrecognized and untreated andropause, many
women are coming into their managerial prime. Both in
business and in bed men feel they can't keep up with
them.

Does this mean that businessmen are now beginning
to feel sexually harassed? Well, probably not in the UK,
but in America increasing numbers of men claim to be
and lawyers specializing in this new crime are thriving.
This may be partly because the American female is
supposed to be more emancipated and 'up-front' about
her sexual needs than her British counterpart. Then
there is the interesting research finding that more confident and dominant women show higher levels of testosterone than less assertive, stay at home types.

Even male politicians, who by tradition enjoy and
take full advantage of the aphrodisiac of power, are

now feeling more threatened. The more politically correct Labour Party in Britain is introducing positive discrimination in favour of women in the selection of parliamentary candidates and ministers for shadow cabinet posts.

With all this pressure on men, no wonder the male mid-life crisis is striking with increasing frequency and severity. Suicide rates in men, always more frequent than in women, are increasing rapidly. A recent study in Britain by the Samaritans organization called *Behind the Mask* showed that over the last 15 years women's suicide rates had halved, while men are four times as likely to take their own lives, especially between the ages of 35 and 44, the peak mid-life crisis years.

Apart from their higher suicide rates, more men die from accidents at all ages, particularly when young, from road traffic injuries. Also, though women generally complain more about their health, the number of life-threatening illnesses they suffer is generally less than the male, and more is spent on their health care. In Britain, as in all developed countries around the world, including the USA, large amounts of money are spent on screening for cancers of the breast and cervix, which are decreasing, while men have virtually nothing spent on detecting prostatic or testicular cancers, which are becoming more common.

As a result of these combined factors, the life expectancy of men in most Western countries, including the UK and USA, is seven to eight years fewer than that of women. Is this an unalterable fact of life or would better health care for men, including hormone replacement therapy with testosterone, narrow the gap? We should urgently be trying to find out.

One of the countries with the lowest gap in life expectancies is Greece. Greek men also have one of the lowest heart attack rates in Europe. Though this is doubtless partly due to the benefits attributed to a 'Mediterranean diet', there would seem to be other psychological and cultural factors at work also. It is worth looking to see what we might learn from their experience, without holding it up as ideal, desirable or even practical for most men.

In Greece the birth of a male child is a matter for great rejoicing, whereas the parents receive sympathy when a girl is born. Sons are the centre of attention in the family, and are spoiled continuously and indulged by their mothers, sisters and grandmothers. At school the boys are outgoing and develop a wide circle of friends, which during adolescence form a supportive in-group, or *parea*, who stand by each other loyally for the rest of their lives. Youthful depression and suicide are relatively rare, though road accidents, drugs and AIDS are taking an increasing toll. Marriage tends to be late and to a considerably younger woman, and according to the Greek Orthodox tradition, divorce is relatively rare. Partly this is due to having a well-worn escape route down to the local *cafeneon*, where a man can be comforted by his all-male support group.

Unlike the majority of British men, with their usual constant distant manner and stiff upper lip, physical contact and letting their feelings out is part of the way of life for Greek men at all ages. Both men and women sing, dance, laugh, weep, hug, kiss and literally pat each other on the back at every opportunity. As well as being in touch physically, they enjoy eloquent, spirited, emotionally charged conversations punctuated by laughter and decorated with gesture. Being cool, cut-off and alone are thought to lead to loneliness, which is considered to be the worst of human afflictions, whereas good company, together with food and wine, is the elixir of life.

The Greek man often does more than one job, which tends to keep him active and employed to a respected and ripe old age. Late in life he is lovingly supported by his wife, sisters, daughters and daughters-in-laws and generally cared for at home until he dies. This life-long pattern keeps his testosterone and level of sexual activity high throughout.

A recent study of young Greek soldiers showed levels of testosterone right at the upper limit of normal and very high rates of sexual activity, with one ejaculation per day on average. This seemed to be proportional to the amount of dihydrotestosterone (DHT), one of the breakdown products of testosterone, rather than testosterone itself. However this may have been a result rather than a cause of their vigorous sex lives and doesn't agree with other evidence that suggests that testosterone is more important in regulating libido.

At the other end of the scale you have the former Greek Prime Minister, with the appropriately doubly, if not trebly, androgenic name of Andreas Papandreou, who in his eighties scandalized his nation by marrying an airline stewardess in her twenties.

This does not mean that I recommend such drastic remedies to my patients or that such idyllic female support as Greek men traditionally enjoy is widely available in most men's lives, but I do think that there are important lessons to be learned from Greek male life patterns, and you will hear them echoed throughout this discussion on how to retain vitality and virility.

The Flight Plan for Life

Life can be compared to a trip in a glider when, after being catapulted in our teens and early twenties to the peak of our innate physical and mental abilities by a powerful cocktail of hormones, including particularly testosterone and oestrogen, we then go into a variable glide path for the rest of our lives, the rate of descent largely being controlled by the body's hormonal balance.

As already explained, some hormones, particularly the stress hormones such as adrenaline, noradrenaline and cortisol, increase wear and tear and the rate at which we use up our energy, having what is known as a catabolic (or breakdown) action. Others, particularly testosterone and oestrogen, have the opposite, or what is called anabolic (or build-up) effect. This can explain why some people burn themselves out and go into a nose-dive, their health crashing at the age of 50 or earlier, while others glide gently on into their 80s or even 100.[1]

These ageing processes affect particularly the heart and blood vessels and, in the form of heart attacks and strokes, are the number one killer of Westerners, as I described in *The Western Way of Death: Stress, tension and heart disease*. Coronary heart disease is also the main reason why, on average, the life expectancy of men in Western society is so much less than that of women.[2]

In general, both physically and mentally, you're as young as your arteries. So, as testosterone and oestrogen have both been used to prevent and treat heart and circulatory disease, and also maintain the condition of the skin, muscles and bones, it seems reasonable to expect that we could use them to slow down the ageing processes and prolong active and enjoyable life.

Age, stress, alcohol and drugs are, as already discussed, the main factors in bringing on the andropause, so any plan to maintain vitality and virility must take these into account. Though you can do this on your own with the help of this book, it is much better to have a medical adviser to guide you individually. At the risk, as elsewhere in this book, of offending the politically correct lobby, I would suggest this adviser should be male, and probably in his forties, fifties or sixties so that he has plenty of experience and knowledge of the problems, having successfully solved many of them himself. Ideally he should be one of that currently rare breed, the andrologist, with a broad range of postgraduate training and specialist interest in endocrinology as it applies to men, as well as knowledge of fertility, erectile and psycho-sexual problems. Alternatively, an experienced general practitioner who has read widely on the subject, particularly if he has attended courses on the more specialist areas of andrology, could be a good adviser. Perhaps most important of all is to find one you can confide in and relate to, and whose opinion you respect.

Whoever you chose, he should be able to tell whether you are going through a mid-life crisis or male menopause and to help you through both. In other words, by a review of your long-term health record, together with how you feel and how you function, and by a detailed medical screen as described in the previous chapter, you can find out which glide path you're on and what flight corrections are needed. Many of these corrections will be self-evident while others will need a more objective or detailed analysis by your medical adviser.

Slowing Ageing

A population peak of 'Baby Boomers' is now reaching the age of 50. This affluent group has generally more leisure and disposable income than earlier generations and is tending to retire earlier. They therefore have higher expectations for the quality of their lives from 50 onwards and are unwilling to tolerate passively the symptoms of the menopause, male or female. Having the wealth, they want the health and happiness to go with it in what should be the 'golden years'.

Health maintenance, or what used to be called preventive medicine, is a relatively undeveloped and unsuccessful science, at least as far as the middle and later years are concerned. Coronary prevention studies such as the Multiple Risk Factor Intervention Trial, mistermed MR FIT, have generally proved uniformly unsuccessful, any small reduction in heart disease being outweighed by increased deaths from accidental deaths and suicides.

Similarly, as an article in *The Times*, 'Behind the Screens', recently pointed out, routine medical screens, though seeming like a good idea at the time, and taking up considerable private and public resources, have not in fact made any appreciable impact on either morbidity or mortality in any area, especially cancer. Indeed, as this thought-provoking article points out, by causing needless expensive and anxiety provoking further tests, and causing investigation and treatment related disease, screening has so far done virtually nothing to either add years to life or life to years.

There are, however, some rays of hope on this otherwise gloomy scene. We need to look in some new directions. Here are some of the most promising.

Hormone Replacement Therapy

To slow down the ageing process is a combined operation. As already stated, you need to promote those activities which maintain, build up or restore mental and physical function, and reduce those which cause wear and tear and breakdown. While there is of course much more to ageing than hormonal decline, I believe there is a strong case for promoting and prolonging a youthful balance of hormones by careful supplementation of the 'hormones of youth', i.e. oestrogens in women and testosterone in men.

The safety and effectiveness of carefully and cautiously applied testosterone treatment has already been described in detail. It shares many of the benefits of oestrogen therapy, both in the treatment of symptoms of the menopause and in all-round mental and physical health maintenance. Both oestrogen and testosterone can be regarded as anabolic or build-up steroids.

If the woman in a man's life is either younger than him in terms of years or hormonally younger because of hormone replacement therapy, it seems to help to keep him young also. This is provided the gap between the two is not so great that the bridge falls down.

'His and hers hormones' are certainly usually preferable to a man getting a divorce and marrying a much younger woman in order to regain his lost youth. Apart from the pain to the former spouse and the rest of the family, there is the emotional, social and financial stress caused to the man involved, the most painful part often being separation from his children. Though the new marriage may appear to be working for a year or two, as the divergence in interests and energy levels becomes more marked, the much older man is usually left trailing mentally, physically and, perhaps most important, sexually, and the relationship often falls apart with extreme unhappiness on both sides.

Attitude to ageing is also important. With improved health care throughout life, especially with HRT, women are coming to expect to remain mentally and physically active, and to look and feel good, for longer and longer.

They see celebrities such as Joan Collins, Catherine Deneuve and Elizabeth Taylor looking as young and attractive in their fifties and sixties as they did in their forties, and have similar expectations for themselves. Increasingly men are having to think seriously about how they are going to keep up with their hormonally reactivated wives.

Some just give up and become couch potatoes, slumped inert in front of the television. Others try to rise to the occasion by going on a diet, giving up smoking and joining a gym or playing more sport, but these efforts often fade rapidly, given the negative mood and inertia accompanying the andropause. Maintaining a positive attitude is an important part of the 'flight plan for life' and this is greatly helped by testosterone treatment.

Stress Management

Stress is one of the major factors contributing to the andropause and, as already described, works against testosterone both by reducing its production and by releasing stress hormones such as adrenaline, noradrenaline and cortisol, which have a catabolic action. It is important, therefore, that as part of your flight plan you become aware of your 'stress payload' and how well or badly you are handling it.

This is not to suggest that you should become a stress-avoiding vegetable. Stress has had a bad press, but it can in fact be the spice of life and a certain amount is essential for our health.

The original definition of stress in engineering terms is: *'a force which when applied to a body sets up strains within it'*. So stress can be seen as a very necessary force which powers our lives. It is related to pleasure, performance and productivity by an inverted U-shaped curve, which varies from person to person. In just the right amounts, what could be called the 'work-out' sector of the curve, the upper half of the left-hand part, stress makes us fizz and function at an optimal level.

Where the bad image of stress arises is when the amount increases to the point where we are pushed over the peak of the curve into the slippery slope of the 'burn-out' sector on the right-hand side. We may then blow a mental fuse and have a nervous breakdown or slide into a depression, or a physical fuse and have a heart attack or develop a stomach ulcer.[3] Some people, notably certain politicians, can carry huge amounts of stress, while other, more sensitive souls, who are often creative and artistic, finding high-stress situations difficult or impossible to cope with.

Stress is actually very addictive, a big turn on, and the common chemical pathway to pleasure is the stress hormone noradrenaline. This is released by what I call the 'six-C situations': competition, car-driving, cigarette smoking, caffeine consumption, cold bracing conditions and copulation or other vigorous physical activity. This has been confirmed by blood samples taken in all these situations.[4] In my early days of stress research, my cardiologist friend Dr Peter Taggart and I found *Guinness Book of Records* levels of noradrenaline in the blood of racing drivers immediately after a race, especially where they did well, though it was difficult to catch up with them later to study the other situations mentioned.[5]

If you have too little stress or stimulation in your life, you find yourself at the 'rust-out' point at the bottom left-hand side of the curve. This is seen in the unemployed, those made redundant and in some people who have to retire earlier than they feel they should. Rust-out can be just as much a cause of 'distress' as burn-out, and may be one of the reasons why there is more social unrest and crime in times of recession, when the devil is making work for idle hands.

It is easier to tell when we are under-stimulated and bored then when we are overloaded with stress. We tend to overlook the early warning signs of excess stress, such as falling function and no fun in work and social life, anxiety and depression, poor sleep and migraine or tension headaches, hypertension, raised blood cholesterol, eczema, asthma and a variety of other psychosomatic ailments.

Avoiding Burn-Out

What can we do to reduce our chances of getting into this over-stressed, 'burn-out' state?

First, we can try 'stress reduction', that is, how we can reduce unnecessary and unenjoyable forms of stress as far as possible. Some work related and family related stresses are unavoidable, but others just pile up unnoticed over time and can be weeded out when you think about them or write them down as a 'Stress Inventory'. Some are just due to trying to cram too many things into the day and so choices have to be made. Some are due to hard-driving time and deadline conscious Type-A behaviour patterns or 'hurry disease' as described by the American cardiologist Dr Ray Rosenman in his book *Type-A Behaviour and your Heart*, in which he gives Type-A drills to modify this harmful lifestyle.[6] The 'time management' skills taught in business school can come in useful here.

Avoiding people and situations which we recognize as being stressful to us can also be helpful. There is a certain type of person who is a 'stress carrier', rather like 'Typhoid Mary'. Though such people usually show no signs of being stressed themselves, they leave a trail of devastation behind them in the form of over-stressed people. As one American admiral put it when asked how he coped with the stress of his job, *'I don't take it in – I dish it out!'*

How can you cope with these people? Sometimes you can avoid them like the plague they are and not be around when they call. Others are just unavoidable, but you may be able to explain to them the way they make you feel and work out a way in which your contacts with them can become less stressful. A very good manual of survival strategies in this situation is *Nasty People: How to stop being hurt by them without becoming one of them* by Jay Carter.[7] Transactional Analysis skills as described in the books of the American psychologist Eric Byrne, especially *The Games People Play*,[8] can also help defuse and prevent tension arising from contact with stress carriers.

The car is also a great stress-generating machine, as my research into stress hormone levels in different situations showed. The racing drivers' noradrenaline had the effect of raising blood fat levels, particularly neutral fat or triglyceride, so that the blood plasma became opalescent and milky after the race.[9] We also found that even in everyday motoring, noradrenaline and adrenaline levels shot up in most drivers, particularly when getting angry with other drivers, snarled up in a traffic jam or fined for parking. As I described in *The Western Way of Death*, men particularly are very attached to their 'ego chariots', and 'machismo machines'. You see rage reactions in and around cars during bumper-to-bumper mortal combat in traffic that you seldom see in other situations.[10]

At work, pecking order equals parking order. It is worth considering whether you can let the train take the strain for some of the intercity journeys or travelling to work, or let the cabby's coronaries take the strain for getting around town. Again, society has a part to play here in encouraging governments to improve public transport and thereby limit both pollution of the external environment by exhaust fumes from the traffic that clogs our roads and of our internal environment from the stress related fats which clog our arteries.

Accidents are another source of stress and rapid ageing, very often related to Type-A behaviour, stress, tranquillizer use, drinking and driving, both on the road, at work and in the home. You may have seen in friends or relations how much a serious accident can age a person. Careful and cautious driving, as taught by the Institute of Advanced Motorists in Britain, in cars with all the latest safety features, is to be recommended in avoiding accelerated ageing.

My research on the effects of major trauma showed very high levels of stress hormones and marked lowering of testosterone levels, which reached crisis point about a week after the accident and could cause delayed deaths at that time from multiple organ damage, especially to the heart and brain.[11] Some of these effects could be reduced by stress-blocking drugs such as the beta-blockers. Many of my patients dated the sudden onset of their andropausal symptoms to an accident or major operation, particularly involving surgery of the heart or prostate gland, so the fewer the operations you have the better.

Among its other advantages, so-called 'key-hole surgery', using endoscopic instruments, may help to minimize operative trauma, post-operative complications and immobility, thereby lessening the wear and tear associated with operations, especially in the elderly. Also by reducing osteoporosis, testosterone is likely to make the trauma of hip, and other fractures less likely.

Stone Age Reactions to Stress

We have not changed essentially in our mental and physical constitution for thousands of years. Modern Space Age man still has his Stone Age psychology, physiology, biochemistry and endocrinology. His hormonal responses to a stressful situation are still the same whether it's fighting a hostile take-over bid in the board-room or a sabre-toothed tiger in the jungle. In either stressful situation the primitive fight-flight mechanism comes into action, and the body is put into a state of emergency by the autonomic or automatic nervous system and the associated hormones.

How does this happen? Adrenaline speeds up the heart and mobilizes sugar into the bloodstream, while noradrenaline produces arousal, and raises blood pressure and fat levels to pump these fuels into the muscles, giving extra energy for fighting or running away. At the same time that these breakdown, catabolic processes are being switched on, the build-up, anabolic processes linked with testosterone are being switched off, because this is a time to make war, not love.

The problem in modern times is that our instinctual reactions to stress have become inappropriate. Much as we might feel like it, when in danger, when in doubt, we can't scream and shout and run about.

Let's look at the various ways in which we can balance up our stress responses.

Exercise

Physical exercise is one of the best and most natural ways of getting our mental and physical reactions to stress back into balance again. After exercise, the mind calms down, the tension in the previously coiled springs of the muscles is reduced, and the sugars and fats mobilized into the bloodstream have been used up. In this state of rest, relaxation and restoration, testosterone levels rise again, as has been shown in many research studies on people exercising. If you overdo it, however, and the exercise itself is pushed to the point where it becomes stressful, testosterone levels fall, as was shown in marathon runners. So, train, don't strain, and remember, exercise doesn't have to hurt to do you good – quite the reverse. No pain means safer gain!

With this in mind, and because the andropause is mainly a condition seen in men around the age of 50, exercise in this group should be designed according to the acronym SAFE. It stands for Safe, Acceptable, Fitness producing and Economic, and is fully described in the book *F/40: Fitness on Forty Minutes a Week* Al Murray and I wrote together.[12] . . . Here is a summary:

S – *Safety* is the essential requirement for exercise in this age group of men. It should ideally be vigorous but not violent, calming and not over-competitive, and isotonic, or dynamic, rather than isometric, or static, which causes the blood pressure to rise too much. A good safety check is the pulse rate, which can be taken by feeling it at the wrist or using a pulse monitor. This should not rise above a safe level, which can be calculated according to your age, fitness and medical condition.

A – *Acceptability* is essential as it is no use having the best system of exercises in the world if you never use it. Find the form of exercise you find acceptable to you and use that. The right surroundings are important. If you don't feel like going to a gym or swimming pool, a personal fitness trainer in your home may be the answer, as well as providing the necessary motivation.

F – *Fitness* in terms of feeling and looking better, and

greater strength and mobility, together with the relief or prevention of andropausal symptoms, are some of the benefits of exercise. These can be especially marked during treatment with testosterone.

E – *Economy* both in terms of time and money is attractive to most people taking up exercise. Two 20-minute periods of vigorous exercise each week, or three times that amount of light exercise, are sufficient for most men to maintain a reasonable level of fitness, control weight, raise testosterone levels and keep sexually active.

Having covered the basic principles of exercise to maintain vitality and virility, let's take specific examples:

- Walking – This, like cycling, is a much underestimated and under-used form of exercise which can not only be used to replace much stressful driving, but is a good basis on which to get fit enough for more vigorous physical activity. To give maximum benefit it needs to be brisk enough to raise the pulse rate to over 100 beats per minute, at least in the unfit. This means really striding out, what I call 'power walking'. Twenty minutes of this daily will give a good level of fitness in most men over the age of 50.

- Golf can also be a good way to encourage walking in pleasant company, providing it does not become too competitive. Unless you find walking very difficult for any reason, beware the buggy, which can spoil the exercise element in golf. Many patients find that testosterone treatment reduces their golf handicap, improves their concentration and strengthens their drive *(see Alan's story, pages 117–18)*. Perhaps one day golf clubs will have to have special competition categories for those on or off anabolic steroids.

- Swimming is excellent whole-body exercise, especially for those trying to lose weight. It could be said that you get 'double-bubble benefit' with swimming, because you are not only burning off a lot of calories by exercising the main muscle masses of the body, but also using up even more in keeping warm because of the heat loss even in water at a comfortable temperature. Unlike land-based exercise, any excess weight is supported in the water and does not throw strain on the joints. It's also a sociable and enjoyable form of exercise, and the sight of a range of attractive women in revealing costumes may do wonders for the libido of the andropausal male.

- Gymnasium exercise is becoming increasingly popular and some enlightened firms are even providing it in-house. Ten years ago, with Al Murray, I helped to establish a gym in the House of Commons to encourage Members of Parliament to be at least physically fit to govern, though it seems to still be seriously under-used. Favoured exercises amongst politicians still seem to be horizontal jogging, running opponents down and leaping to conclusions.

- Good facilities in a gym should include properly trained and experienced instructors who carry out an initial fitness assessment, including measurements of heart attack risk factors such as blood pressure, and keep a continuing watchful and encouraging eye on your progress. Exercise schedules should be tailor-made to the individual and progress carefully monitored in terms of 'perceived exertion', i.e. how hard the exercise feels, as well as by pulse rate measurements.[13]

• Straining at heavy weights is to be avoided, as are press-ups. With press-ups you are lifting three-quarters of the body weight and this is too much like maximal isometric exercise. The blood pressure is greatly raised by this type of activity and because of the increased pressure in the chest, blood cannot get back to the heart.

Also to be avoided is prolonged exposure to high temperature sauna baths after exercise. Research we carried out at Al Murray's City Gym in London and reported in the *British Medical Journal*[14] showed that at high temperatures large amounts of adrenaline are released, and can make the heart beat rapidly and erratically. This can be more unsafe than strenuous exercise, particularly in those with high blood pressure or heart trouble. Cold plunges after the sauna are also not a good idea, as we showed that they cause the release of nora-drenaline, which produces a dramatic surge in blood pressure. All these violent circulatory gymnastics are best avoided if you are seriously interested in longevity.

Running and Jogging

Unless you are already in training, running and jogging are generally too vigorous to take up immediately without a period of power walking for several weeks before-hand. Even then these forms of exercise have been accused of 'mass murder' by Dr Meyer Friedman, a leading American cardiologist, who would agree with the cautionary saying, *'The grim reaper also wears a tracksuit.'* One of his recent victims was Jim Fix, the American running populist, who abruptly dropped dead in his tracks, and he also obviously had designs on several American Presidents, who tend to overdo the fitness kick. Carter had to be carted off from one run, Bush was so bushed on another he collapsed and Clinton is visibly declining every time he is seen jogging. They must have got confused at an early age about the literal and metaphorical meaning of Presidents needing to run for office. Either that or they are running scared of the 25th Amendment to the American Constitution, introduced after the cover up of President Dwight Eisenhower's stroke in the 1950s, in which a President can be declared unfit to govern for health reasons.

Apart from the dangers to the heart and circulation in running, in some cities there is an increasing chance of actually being run over. Getting mugged is another risk. Knee and ankle injuries are also common, and running on hard pavements has been shown to cause blood to appear in the urine from trauma to the kidneys. As with walking, well designed shoes with shock absorbent insoles are vital for both safety and comfort.

Mental Exercise as an Antidote to Stress

While many doctors know about meditation in relieving anxiety, few realize just how powerful a tool it can be in stress management. Lectures in medical school mainly tend to focus on the wonders of medication, giving a message which is reinforced throughout the medical career by bombardment with literature and free samples from the drug companies. There are so many drugs to regulate our mental state on the market now that you might be forgiven for wondering if any of them work effectively. Also, there are many worrying reports of side-effects.

Stress related symptoms are actually trying to warn us of something and taking medication is often just like turning off the fire alarm because you don't like the noise of the bells. Many patients tell of a zombie-like, switched-off state they experience on tranquillizers.

Malcolm Lader, Professor of Psychopharmacology in the leading research centre in the field, the Institute of Psychiatry in London, has reported on the severe habituation which comes with long-term tranquillizer use, their addictive properties and the acute withdrawal symptoms which occasionally occur with suddenly coming off them. He also created alarm and despondency among doctors and patients alike when he reported that CAT scans showed that long-term tranquillizer use caused shrinkage of the brain similar to that seen in alcoholics, apparently due to 'neuronal drop-out'.

Given such information, many people would prefer to control the stress in their lives by meditation rather than medication. It can be very effective in the control of stress reactions, whether as one of the different types of yoga or in its modern Western forms.

Meditation is simply the direction of flow of attention, according to Patanjali, the eighth-century Indian sage who systematized yoga. Most of the time our attention is directed outwardly. This focuses it on all the different forms of stress in our lives. In susceptible people it creates a vicious circle of stress leading to increasing stress hormones and decreasing testosterone, which all cause symptoms which generate more stress and further unfavourable hormonal changes.

When attention is directed inwardly, which is what people usually understand by meditation, we become uncoupled from the stresses in our lives and the body's self-healing, restorative relaxation responses take over.

This produces a switch from over-activity of the fight-flight 'war' system to increased activity of the rest-restore-relaxation 'peace' system, with corresponding hormonal benefits, including the restoration of testosterone levels.

Such voluntary control over the body's involuntary nervous system, the autopilot which regulates our responses to stress, is remarkably easy to achieve. There is a whole range of techniques to help, which originated with yoga methods in India, moved to China as Buddhist meditation and then to Japan as Zen meditation.[15]

Autogenic Training is a Westernized rediscovery of the basic principles of Eastern forms of meditation. Its essential basis is the sequence of the six standard exercises developed 60 years ago by Dr Johannes Schultz, a German psychiatrist working in Berlin, where an institute has been dedicated to his memory. Autogenic Training involves focusing the mind by silent repetition of 'verbal formulae' suggesting sensations of heaviness and warmth in the arms and legs, a calm regular heartbeat, easy natural breathing, abdominal warmth and cooling of the forehead.

Under medical supervision, these mental exercises are progressively introduced at individual or small-group training sessions held once a week over an eight to ten-week period. The patients then practise them in a comfortable, stable, sitting position on the edge of a chair, in an armchair or lying flat-out on their backs. Whether at home, in the office or travelling, they can usually find an opportunity for a session of 'Autogenics'. Usually the recommended practice time is 10 to 15 minutes three or four times a day.

You don't have to be a burnt-out stress victim to benefit from Autogenic Training. It has been widely used in industry and, being non-competitive and non-intrusive, can be taught on in-house courses. It has also been taught to airline pilots and has proved helpful in coping with jet-lag. It was one factor that the training of both astronauts and cosmonauts had in common. It has also been used extensively with competitive sportsmen and women, together with musicians and others in the performing arts. There are many fringe benefits, such as reducing the amount of sleep required and promoting creative thinking by balancing up the two sides of the brain, the logical, linear-thinking left and the intuitive, creative right.[16]

For the andropausal patient, as well as reducing stress, Autogenic Training can help control alcohol and food intake gently but firmly over a period of weeks. The psychological effects can also help the person sort out long-standing emotional problems both at home and at work. However, it must be emphasized that it is a practical skill, like learning to drive a car, and you need a well-trained instructor. Autogenic Training is relatively unknown outside Europe, but Britain is fortunate to have an organization called the British Association for Autogenic Training and Therapy (BAFATT), which can provide a list of trainers in most areas of the UK.[17] It is part of an organization called the International Committee for Autogenic Therapy, dedicated to making properly taught Autogenic Training available round the world.

Siddha meditation is the one Eastern technique of which I have practical experience and can warmly recommend as being a very straightforward form of meditation. It is based on an ancient tradition and philosophies which help control and reduce stress, among its many other life-enhancing benefits.[18] It is a very spontaneous and easy to learn form of meditation, which is taught in over 600 centres all over the world, including North and South America, Britain and the rest of Europe, and Australia as well as India, where it originated and is respected as a great tradition. There is a branch of the Siddha Yoga Foundation in most countries and a centre in most major cities. The current head of this lineage of meditation teachers is a beautiful Indian teacher called Gurumayi Chidvilasananda, the successor to the revered Swami Muktananda.[19]

The technique basically involves calming the mind by focusing it on a simple word formula or mantra, linked with the breathing. This makes use of the age-old observation that when the mind is disturbed, the breathing is usually disturbed also. Conversely, controlling the breathing can help to control the mind. When the mind goes still, great feelings of peace and calm can arise from within, and subtly but powerfully change the person's life, as I and a number of my patients and friends have found.

Avoiding Rust-Out

Every person has an optimal level of stimulation or stress, and above and below it lie unhappiness. Once our basic survival needs are taken care of, as they increasingly are in most societies, and we have fulfilled our 'biological imperative' by having and bringing up our children, what do we do then?

There is an old saying that what you don't use you lose. This is true in terms of mental, physical and sexual function. You see it every day in people who retire, sink into apathy and often die soon afterwards. It is also seen in younger people made redundant who give up hope and give up trying to get a new job. In this situation it is probably better to do anything than do nothing.

It is one of the tragedies of modern life that there

seems to be polarization of the workforce. At one end you have the over-employed, who are risking burn-out by working longer and harder to keep their jobs in the face of seemingly ever increasing competition, and at the other you have the growing ranks of the rust-outs who are unemployed or have been forced into early retirement by redundancy, rationalization and down-sizing of their firms. Both groups can be equally unhappy, but for opposite reasons.

The Protestant work ethic isn't working any longer either, because it is increasingly absent for a large number of people for a large part of their lives. Over the twentieth century more and more people have moved into urban environments, with a corresponding reduction in manual work. The proportion working in agriculture has fallen, in America for example from about 20 per cent to 2 per cent. The 9–5 till 65 is no longer even the structure of the city-dweller's life any more. What's to take its place?

Beer and circuses were the answer during the decline and fall of the Roman empire, and perhaps beer, games shows and the rest of pulp TV are the modern equivalent. Yet beer, combining the hazards of both alcohol and phytoestrogens, certainly doesn't do much for either vitality or virility, and TV mainly promotes endless unsatisfying consumerism and discontent. What are the alternatives?

It is surprising how little either politicians or sociologists appear to be looking into this question, since it seems that one of the main problems to be faced during the next millennium is that work as we know it today is set to become a luxury item. Perhaps occupation should become our preoccupation. Here are some suggestions to fuel the debate, since they have a bearing on how we face up to both the male mid-life crisis and the andropause. A man without a function, after all, often ceases to function as a man.

Alternatives to Work

Perhaps some of the answers to the problems being created by technology may lie in the applications of technology. For some people loss of a job has meant that they can discover new skills and abilities. They may find a new lease of creative life through the computer and even take to surfing on the Internet.

Others are seeking a low-tech answer and welcome the increased time available to them for pure recreation or self-development in a variety of ways. Some take to the worship of the small spherical object known as the golf-ball, playing two rounds a day every day the weather allows them to. Some take up the search for spiritual enlightenment, and enjoy the structured life and discipline that either a church or yoga and meditation can provide them. Perhaps we need counselling centres to help people find their individual answers, or maybe even your friendly neighbourhood andrologist could give some guidance.

Work Sharing

As the number of hours of work needed to perform various jobs falls due to automation and computerization, so the need to share this now precious commodity increases. The trend towards teleworking makes such sharing potentially easier and more attractive in some areas. This can open up a new career working from home via modems, faxes and video-conferencing, without the expenditure of time, energy and money involved in commuting.

Imagine a system where the norm was a 16-hour working week, either two eight-hour days or preferably four four-hour shifts. If you were a morning person, you could leap out of bed and work in the morning. An evening person could surface more gently and work in the afternoons. Moonlighting workaholics would be gently weaned off their addiction in work-withdrawal programmes, led by teams of easy-going idlers. They would be reminded that the working-day of the caveman was only three or four hours long and the rest of the time was spent in social activities such as tribal dancing or personal grooming before an evening round the camp-fire.

Work Shortening

Not only might the working week be shortened, but the years worked might be shortened to 30 or even 20. The Brahmin ideal of life in India has four approximately 20-year periods: student, householder, progressive detachment and ultimate contentment. Having finished your education around the age of 20, you would then have the privilege of working for 20 years to establish your position in a less competitive society, bring up your family, if you decided you wanted one, and have some extra consumer goodies above the guaranteed social norm.

After your 20 years' work, the mid-life crisis would be much less of a problem, because it would be expected that you would take up some more creative or leisurely pastime or study. Rather than 'retiring', you would be advancing in some new direction and might wish to take a few years to attend a 'University of Mid-life' as a mature student to go deeper into something that you might have missed out on previously. (The Open

University in Britain is an encouraging development that many people faced with early loss of employment have found, often to their surprise, gives them a new and absorbing view on life.)

This period of detachment could also lead to more unpaid voluntary work in the community, and perhaps be a time for some to do more social work or counselling. Some could even take up political pursuits, having had more life experience and with more maturity than the average career politician. It may be, however, by this time a person will have come to the same conclusion as the philosopher who set out as a young man to change the world and with increasing experience progressively narrowed his activity to changing his community, to changing his family and friends, to finally just trying to change himself.

Work Shifting

There are some jobs, mainly in the so-called service industries, that just can't be automated. These range from psychotherapy to hairdressing, i.e. sorting out the inside and outside of the head, and from medicine to massage, i.e. making the inside and outside of the body feel better. Shifting work into these often overstretched professions would create many new satisfying jobs, and could well improve the sum of human health and happiness.

For those who wished a more action-packed time in their lives, short periods of voluntary overseas service in teaching survival skills or bringing aid to developing countries or disaster-stricken areas might provide the ideal opportunity.

Power-Sharing

A study of the health of London civil servants, the Whitehall Study, which has been going on for about 30 years, has shown that those in senior positions, the 'mandarins', enjoy better health and tend to live longer than those in the middle or lower echelons. Perhaps the answer to this interesting observation lies in the original meaning of the word 'mandarin', which was 'a high civil servant thought to exercise wide undefined powers outside political control'. The power element may well be linked to testosterone levels, because, as we have seen, the sense of power promotes secretion of this hormone. This is seen throughout the animal kingdom, but particularly in ageing stags, bull-seals and male primates.

Taking this idea a step further, sharing power and empowering people in different areas of their lives could well help to maintain their hormone levels. This would range from setting up managerial structures with a broader power base to setting up production lines, as in the Volvo experiment in Sweden, where one worker sees his product through as from one end to the other, rather than performing one limited task only. Similarly, the American telecommunications company AT & T has extended the powers of an increasing number of their operatives to follow up and provide a larger range of services to the customer who first contacts them and becomes 'their client'.

The rapid improvement in communications may also empower people by letting them take part in decision-making processes at both a local and national level. Via telephone and fibre-optic links they could make their views felt in polls and referenda, and even add a new dimension to the deliberations of their governments by voting live on issues which concern them, making democracy a more exciting, interactive process. It is a frustrating sight to see the often low level of interest and poor attendance rates in parliamentary debates. Immediate feedback on politicians' often dismal performance from the general public might revitalize them.

Alcohol

Alcohol is one of the major factors contributing to the male menopause and if there is a serious alcohol problem it is not worth giving testosterone until it has been treated with the help of one of the effective agencies such as Alcoholics Anonymous. Also, as already described, the testis is very sensitive to both the short and long-term effects of alcohol, even in amounts which are insufficient to damage the liver or cause social problems.

Because of general insecurity, greater unemployment in young people and a general sense of aimlessness and disillusion, the consumption of both alcohol and potentially testicle-damaging drugs such as cannabis is increasing among young men. The average alcohol intake of men aged 18–24 in Britain is now 22 units per week, just above the 21 units which used to be the safety guideline set by the Health Education Council, though this has now, incorrectly I think from the point of view of testicular function, been reset at 28 units. This means that over half of them are at risk of damaging their health, particularly their sexual health, including fertility, by their drinking habits. Also, the most common drink in this age group is beer, the drink most likely to damage the testis and feminize the male. There is a serious warning in the British Health Education Council message that 'There is one part all beers will reach.'

Because of these sobering facts, I usually recommend a return to well within the 21 units of alcohol per week limit. Sometimes the patients find even less is better. Also, because of the phyto-oestrogens in beer, which may still be present even in low alcohol types, it seems worth trading the beer intake for wine, especially red wine.

Diet

Weight reduction is often needed to help in the treatment of andropausal symptoms. In fact weight gain which doesn't respond to diet is one of the most common and demoralizing effects of this condition. Often this is mainly in the lower abdomen, giving a 'beer belly'. One witty journalist said that till the age of 40 he used to be proud of the breadth of his mind and the narrowness of his waist. Then he woke up one morning and found they had changed places.

The spreading waistline is both a sign of the andropause and makes it more severe. This female type of fat distribution is partly due to the action of the oestrogenic factors which may have helped to produce it in the first place and partly because when there is more fat in the body, resistance to the action of testosterone increases and more of it is converted to oestrogen. Testosterone deficiency also causes more sugar and protein to be converted to fat, so there is a general tendency to put on weight. As the couch potato grows, energy decreases, less exercise is taken and, lacking both activity and testosterone drive to build them up, the abdominal muscles melt away as the paunch appears.

Fortunately, as well as restoring the will-power, or rather the won't-power, needed for successful dieting, TRT improves sugar metabolism so that less is converted to fat and more goes to rebuilding the muscles. The effectiveness of this form of treatment was shown in a study in Göteborg in Sweden, where the cosmetic effect in reducing beer bellies, as well as the other benefits of testosterone treatment, was greatly appreciated by both the patients and their partners.

As with alcohol related problems, expert guidance in specialist groups such as Weight Watchers or in the many health clinics specializing in this area may be needed to help the patient really tackle his weight problem, especially after many years of inertia. Where there is marked obesity, this can be a very important factor contributing to resistance to the action of testosterone, essentially similar to the insulin resistance seen in adult onset diabetes.

On a related topic, psychopharmacology is making rapid advances in the field of so-called 'smart drugs' which claim to slow mental ageing and the loss of memory which goes with it. These widely discussed but little applied drugs, combined with psychotherapeutic mental exercises and relaxation techniques, and the benefits of HRT in both sexes on cerebral function and circulation, should have enormous potential in 'brain maintenance'.

Various dietary supplements are on the market, which are claimed to increase libido and help avoid prostate problems. In particular there is an interesting Swiss Oat preparation which is supposed to free up testosterone by reducing the inhibitory SHBG. This may be one of the natural plant hormones which will find a place in the treatment of patients who want to avoid long-term orthodox hormone treatments.

Antioxidants and Micro Nutrients

Antioxidants, especially Vitamins A, C and E, together with micro nutrients such as selenium and zinc, are now widely discussed and taken, both to improve vitality and potency and to reduce heart disease and cancer. However, this is largely on a haphazard basis, without any medical authority or guidance.

I think there is now compelling evidence that vitamin supplements may have a generally beneficial effect in maintaining health and may well reduce heart disease in the long term. These effects may well be due specifically to their antioxidant effect, perhaps by reducing the so-called 'free radicals' which are supposed to contribute to these conditions.

Zinc is concentrated by the prostate gland, and is an important ingredient of the seminal vesicle fluid which joins the semen as it is pumped through the ejaculatory ducts in the prostate gland. Its function seems to be to activate the sperm, which appear to pump zinc just as the muscles pump iron. Like the vitamins, in sensible amounts it appears non-toxic and may be beneficial.

Men's Lib

What I am advocating is boosting the vitality, strength and longevity of men of all ages, but particularly past the age of 50, to the point where it equals that of women, especially when the latter are on HRT.

This is a physical and mental balancing act to maximize the many benefits of testosterone in men. In no way does this mean testosterone for all, male HRT being only given when needed to treat the male menopause or for long-term health maintenance in older men who choose that option. Generally it involves maintaining the body's natural supply of testosterone, seeing that, like the man, it remains free and active, and that its actions are not blocked by factors such as SHBG, oestrogens or stress.

Men are about 30 years behind women when it comes to HRT for the wide variety of historical, medical and marketing reasons already mentioned. Hopefully they will now catch up rapidly as the male menopause is more widely recognized to be a real condition which can and should be treated, and as the safety, effectiveness and many benefits to physical and mental health of TRT become recognized. I have tried to spell out clearly the primary importance of testosterone in maintaining vitality as well as virility, but we need more doctors with a special interest in men's health issues, willing to act as leaders in the fight for what could be called men's lib.

This is not an anti-feminist movement, but a way of recognizing the need to empower men and help them to remain active and equal partners throughout long and healthy lives. The 'women's lib' movement has helped women achieve social and hormonal emancipation, but the men are now lagging behind. In terms of longevity, women's greater life expectancy, when combined with the tendency for their menfolk to be on average three to five years older, according to actuarial statistics, means women lose their partners an average of 10 years or more before they die, which can make for a sad and lonely end to life.

It was the interest, enthusiasm and favourable experiences of the female public at large which brought in HRT with oestrogens as a treatment for the menopause. But the medical profession only belatedly woke up to the potential of HRT, as did the drug companies. May TRT receive quicker acknowledgement. Encouraging news on this front was provided by *The Times* on

January 11th 1996 when it was stated: *'The medical establishment now accepts that men, like women undergo a menopause. HRT for men is on the way.'* The tide of public opinion is changing.

It is my view that recognition of the reality and importance of the male menopause, together with the present careful research in the rapidly expanding field of hormonal replacement therapy in both sexes, will lay the foundation for preventive medicine in the twenty-first century. I suggest that it is only by such advances that the people in the West during the second half of their lives will achieve the World Health Organization's goal of 'health for all by the year 2000'.

References

Introduction: The Male Menopause Mystery

1 Sheehy, G., *New Passages*. London: HarperCollins, 1996
2 Sheehy, G., 'Is there a male menopause?' *Vanity Fair* 1993; 164
3 Goldman, B., Klatz, R., *Death in the Locker Room: Drugs and Sports*. Chicago, Illinois: Elite Sports Medicine Publications Inc., 1992
4 Korkia, P., Stimson, G. V., *Anabolic Steroid Use in Great Britain: An exploratory investigation*. London: HMSO, 1993
5 Hooper, R., *Medical Dictionary*. London: Murray and Highley, 1798
6 Heller, C. G., Myers, G. B., 'The male climacteric: Its symptomatology, diagnosis and treatment' *JAMA* 1944; 126: 472
7 Editorial, ibid.
8 de Kruif, P., *The Male Hormone: A new gleam of hope for prolonging man's prime of life*. New York: Harcourt, Brace and Company, 1945

9 Skolnick, A. A., 'Is "male menopause" real or just an excuse?' *JAMA* 1994

Chapter One: The Testosterone Story

1 Medvei, V. C., *A History of Endocrinology*. Lancaster, England: MTP Press Ltd, 1982

2 de Kruif, P., *The Male Hormone: A new gleam of hope for prolonging man's prime of life*. New York: Harcourt, Brace and Company, 1945

3 Hamalainen, E., Adlercreutz, H., Puska, P., Pietinen, P., 'Diet and serum sex hormones in healthy men' *J Steroid Biochem* 1984; 20 (1): 459–64

4 Irvine, W., 'John Hunter's Experiments: Evidence of an eye witness. Letter to Professor Thomas Hamilton, University of Glasgow, of 17 June 1771' *Lancet* 1928; 359–60

5 Berthold, A. A., 'Transplantation der Hoden' *Arch Anat Physiol Wiss Med* 1849; 42–6

6 Medvei, op. cit.

7 Editorial, 'The pentacle of rejuvenescence' *BMJ* 1889; 1:1416

8 de Kruif, op. cit.

9 Wright, S., *Applied Physiology*. London: Oxford Medical Publications, 1926

10 Ibid.

11 David, K., Dingemanse, E., Freud, J., Laqueur, E., 'Über krystallinisches männliches Hormon aus Hoden (Testosteron), wirksamer als aus Harn oder aus Cholesterin bereitetes Androsteron' *Hoppe-Seylers Z Physiol Chem* 1935; 233: 282

12 Butenandt, F. J., 'Über die chemische Untersuchung der Sexual-hormone' *Z Angew Chem* 1931; 44: 905–8

13 Butenandt, F. J., Hanish, G., 'Über Testosteron.

Umwanlung des Dehydro-androsterons in Androstendiol und Testosteron: ein Weg zur Darstellung des Testosterons aus Cholesterin' *Hoppe-Seylers Z Physiol Chem* 1935; 237: 89–98

14 Ruzicka, L., Wettstein, A., 'Synthetische Darstellung der Testishhormons, Testosteron (Androsten 3 on 17-ol)' *Helv Chim Acta* 1935; 18: 1264–75

15 Thomas, H. B., Hill, R. T., 'Testosterone propionate and the male climacteric', *Endocrinology* 1940; 26: 953

16 Deansley, R., Parkes, A. S., 'Further experiments on the administration of hormones by the subcutaneous implantation of tablets', *Lancet* 1938; 2: 606–8

17 Handelsman, D., 'Pharmacology of testosterone pellet implants' in Nieschlag, E., Behre, H. M., eds, *Testosterone: Action, deficiency, substitution*. Heidelberg: Springer Verlag, 1990; 136–54

18 Ruzicka, L., Goldburg, M. W., Rosenburg, H. R., 'Herstellung des 17-Methyl-testosterons und anderer Androsten- und Androstanderivative zusammen' *Z P* 1935

19 Nieschlag, E., Behre, H. M., 'Pharmacology and clinical uses of testosterone' in Nieschlag, op. cit., 92–114

20 Heller, C. G., Myers, G. B., 'The male climacteric: Its symptomatology, diagnosis and treatment' *JAMA* 1944; 126: 472–77

21 Reiter, T., 'Treatment of male climacteric by combined implantation' *Practitioner* 1953; 170: 181

22 Reiter, T., 'Testosterone implantation: A clinical study of 240 implantations in ageing males' *Journal of the American Geriatrics Society* 1963; 11: 540–50

23 Reiter, T., 'Testosterone therapy' *British Journal of Geriatric Practice* 1967; 4 (2): 137–40

24 Reiter, T., *Reiter's Treatment of Testosterone Deficiency*. London: Organon Laboratories Ltd, 1965

25 Carruthers, M., Murray, A., *F/40: Fitness on Forty Minutes a Week*. London: Futura, 1976

26 Christiansen J., *The Tvedegaard–Møller Trial: A fight against injustice*. Rosenhilde and Begger Copenhagen: 1960

27 Møller, J., Einfeldt, H., *Testosterone Treatment of Cardiovascular Diseases*. Berlin: Springer Verlag, 1984

28 Møller, J., *Cholesterol: Interactions with testosterone and cortisol in cardiovascular disease*. Berlin: Springer Verlag, 1987

29 Møller, J., *Toxic oral antibiotics in relation to cardiovascular disease*. Munich: ECOMED, 1988

Chapter Two:
The Male Menopause or Andropause

1 Carruthers, M., 'Hormone replacement therapy for men' *RCGP Members Reference Book* 1993; 283–5

2 Bancroft, J., *Human Sexuality and its Problems*. Edinburgh: Churchill Livingstone, 1989

3 Bremner, C., 'Hormone count at root of lawyers' machismo' *Times Tribune*, 9 November 1990

4 Gladue, B. A., 'Aggressive behavioral characteristics, hormones, and sexual orientation in men and women' *Aggressive Behaviour* 1991; 17: 314–26

5 Baucom, D. H., 'Relation between testosterone concentration, sex role identity, and personality among females' *Journal of Personality and Social Psychology* 1985; 48: 1218–26

6 Greer, G., *The Change*. London: Penguin Books, 1992

7 Vermeulen, A., 'Androgens in the ageing male' *Journal of Clinical Endocrinology and Metabolism* 1991; 73: 221–4

8 Lichtenstein, M. J., Yarnell, J. M., Elwood, P. C., *et al.*, 'Sex hormones, insulin, lipids, and prevalent ischemic heart disease' *American Journal of Epidemiology* 1987; 126 (4): 647–57

9 Barrett-Conner, E., Khaw, K., 'Endogenous sex hormones and cardiovascular disease in men: A prospective population-based study' *Circulation* 1988; 78: 539–44

10 Møller, J., Einfeldt, H., *Testosterone Treatment of Cardiovascular Diseases*. Berlin: Springer Verlag, 1984

11 Feldman, J. M., Postlethwaite, R. W., Glenn, J. F., 'Hot flashes and sweats in men with testicular insufficiency' *Arch Intern Med* 1976; 136: 606–8

12 Francis, R. M., Peacock, M., Aaron, J. E., *et al.*, 'Osteoporosis in hypogonadal men: Role of decreased plasma 1,25-dihydroxyvitamin D, calcium malabsorption, and low bone formation' *Bone* 1986; 7: 261–8

13 Kelly, P. J., *et al.*, 'Dietary calcium, sex hormones, and bone mineral density in men' *BMJ* 1990; 300: 1361–4

14 Phillips, S. K., *et al.*, 'Muscle weakness in women occurs at an earlier age than in men, but strength is preserved by hormone replacement therapy' *Clinical Science* 1993; 84: 95–8

Chapter Three: Not the Mid-Life Crisis

1 Brim, O. G., 'Theories of the male mid-life crisis' *Counselling Psychologist* 1976; 6: 2–9

2 Amis, M., *The Information*. London: HarperCollins, 1995

3 Dimbleby, J., *The Prince of Wales: A biography*. London: Little, Brown & Co., 1994

4 Lax, E., *Woody Allen: A biography*. London: Jonathan Cape, 1991

5 Barrymore, M., *Back in Business*. London: Hutchinson, 1995

6 Lewis, R., *The Life and Death of Peter Sellers*. London: Century, 1994

7 Davis, J. H., *The Kennedys: Dynasty and disaster 1848–1983*. New York: McGraw-Hill, 1984

8 Markson, E. W., Gognalons, N. M., 'Midlife: Crisis or nodal point?' in Hess, B., Markson, E. W., eds, *Growing Old in America*. New Brunswick, NJ: Transaction, 1991

9 Jaques, E., 'Death and the mid-life crisis' *Int J Psycho-analysis* 1965; 46: 502–14

Chapter Four: How It Happens

1 Moir, A., Jessel, D., *Brain Sex*. London: Michael Joseph, 1989

2 Gray, Anna, Jackson, Douglas, McKinlay, John B., 'The relation between dominance, anger and hormones in normally aging men: Results from the Massachusetts male aging study' *Psychosomatic Medicine* 1991; 53: 375–85

3 Dabbs, J., De la Rue, D., Williams, P. M., 'Testosterone and occupational choice: Actors, ministers and other men' *Journal of Personality and Social Psychology* 1990; 59: 1261–5

4 Rommerts, F. F. G., 'Testosterone: An overview of biosynthesis, transport, metabolism and action' in Nieschlag, E., Behre, H. M., eds, *Testosterone: Action, deficiency, substitution*. Heidelberg: Springer Verlag, 1990; 1–22

5 Hamalainen, E., Adlercreutz, H., Puska, P., Pietinen, P., 'Diet and serum sex hormones in healthy men'

J Steroid Biochem 1984; 20 (1): 459–64

6 Carruthers, M., *The Western Way of Death: Stress, tension and heart disease*. London and New York: Davis-Poynter and Pantheon Books, 1974

7 Rudman, D., Feller, A. G., Nagraj, H. S., *et al.*, 'Effects of human growth hormone in men over 60 years old' *New England Journal of Medicine* 1990; 323 (1): 1–6

8 Vermeulen, A., 'Androgens and male senescence' in Nieschlag, E., Behre, H. M., eds, *Testosterone: Action, deficiency, substitution*. Heidelberg: Springer Verlag, 1990; 261–76

9 Schmidt, H., Starcevic, Z., 'Urinary testosterone excretion in men at different ages and the causation of testicular insufficiency' *Klin Wschr* 1967; 45: 377–82

10 Neaves, W. B., Johnson, L., Porter, I. C., Parker, C. R., Petty, C. S., 'Leydig cell numbers, daily sperm production and serum gonadotrophin levels in aging men' *J Clin Endocrinol Metab* 1984; 59: 756–63

11 Sparrow, D., Boss, R., Rowe, J. N., 'The influence of age, alcohol consumption and body build on gonadal function in men' *J Clin Endocrinol Metab* 1980; 51: 508–12

12 Plymate, S. R., Tenover, J. S., Bremner, W. J., 'Circadian variations in testosterone, sex hormone binding globulin testosterone in healthy young and elderly men' *J Androl* 1989; 10: 366–71

13 Sharpe, R. M., Skakkebaek, N. E., 'Are oestrogens involved in falling sperm counts and disorders of the male reproductive tract?' *Lancet* 1993; 341: 1392–5

14 Sharpe, R. M., 'Another DDT connection' *Nature* 1995; 375: 538–9

15 Toppari, J., *et al.*, 'Male reproductive health and

environmental chemicals with estrogenic effects' 1995; Miljoprojekt 290: 1–166

16 Carruthers, M., 'The case of the caponized farmers' *Back to Nature* British Andrology Society, 1995

17 Dodds, E. C., Golberg, L., Lawson, W., Robinson, R., 'Oestrogenic activity of certain synthetic compounds' *Nature* 1938; 141: 247–8

18 Dodds, E. C., Golberg, L., Lawson, W., Robinson, R., 'Oestrogenic activity of alkylated stilboestols' *Nature* 1938; 142: 34

19 Kelce, W. R., Stone, C. R., Laws, S. C., Gray, E. L., Kemppainen, J. A., Wilson, E. M., 'Persistent DDT metabolite p,p'-DDE is a potent androgen receptor antagonist' *Nature* 1995; 375: 581–5

20 Steinberger, E., 'The etiology and pathophysiology of testicular dysfunction in man' *Fertil Steril* 1978; 29: 481–91

21 Wolnisty, C., 'Orchitis as a complication of infectious mononucleosis' *New England Journal of Medicine* 1962; 266: 88

22 Hubert, W., 'Psychotropic effects of testosterone' in Nieschlag, E., Behre, H. M., eds, *Testosterone: Action, deficiency, substitution*. Heidelberg: Springer Verlag, 1990; 51–71

23 Arguelles, A. E., Carruthers, M. E., Mosovich, A., 'Man in transit: Biochemical and physiological changes during intercontinental flights' *Lancet* 976; 1: 977–81

24 Poggi, U. L., Arguelles, A. E., Rosner, J., *et al.*, 'Plasma testosterone and serum lipids in male survivors of myocardial infarction' *Journal of Steroid Biochemistry* 1976; 7: 229–31

25 Kreuz, L. E., Rose, R. M., Jennings, J. R., 'Suppression of plasma testosterone levels and psychological stress' *Arch Gen Psychiat* 1972; 26: 479–82

26 Mazur, A., Lamb, T. A., 'Testosterone, status and mood in human males' *Horm Behav* 1980; 14: 236–46

27 Fox, C. A., Ismail, A. A., Love, D. N., Kirkham, K. E., Loraine, J. A., 'Studies on the relationship between plasma testosterone levels and human sexual activity' *J Endocrinol* 1996; 52: 51–8

28 Mathur, R. S., Neff, M. R., Landgreve, S. C., 'Time-related changes in the plasma concentrations of prolactin, gonadotrophins, sex hormone binding globulin, and certain steroid hormones in female runners after a long distance race' *Fertil Steril* 1986; 6: 1067–70

29 Van Thiel, D., Lester, R., 'The effect of chronic alcohol abuse on sexual function' *Clinics in Endocrinology and Metabolism* 1979; 8: 499–510

30 Sparrow, *et al.*, op. cit.

31 Cornaro, L., *Sure Methods of Attaining a Long and Healthfull Life*. 1530

32 Parazzini, F., *et al.*, 'Tight underpants and trousers and risk and dyspermia' *Int J Androl* 1995; 18: 137–40

33 Ando, S., *et al.*, 'The influence of age on Leydig cell function in patients with varicocele' *Int J Androl* 1996; 7: 104–18

Chapter Five:
Vasectomy: The Unkindest Cut of All

1 Goldstein, M., Feldberg, M., *The Vasectomy Book: A complete guide to decision making*. Wellingborough, Northamptonshire: Turnstone Press, 1985

2 Ibid.

3 Wolfers, D., Wolfers, H., *Vasectomy and Vasectomania*. London: Mayflower Books Ltd, 1974

4 Hodgekinson, N. *It's Safer to Wait. Daily Mail*, April 4th 1979.

5 Nirapathpongporn, A., Huber, D. H., Krieger, J. N., 'No-scalpel vasectomy at the King's birthday vasectomy festival' *Lancet* 1990; 335: 894–5

6 McMahon, A. J., Buckley, J., Taylor, A., Lloyd, S. N., Deane, R. F., Kirk, D., 'Chronic testicular pain following vasectomy' *Br J Urol* 1992; 69: 188–91

7 Chen, T. F., Ball, R. Y., 'Epididymectomy for post-vasectomy pain: Histological review' *Br J Urol* 1991; 68: 407–13

8 Fowler, J. E. Jr, Mariano, M., 'Immunoglobulin in seminal fluid of fertile, infertile, vasectomy and vasectomy reversal patients' *J Urol* 1983; 129: 869–72

9 Isidori, A., Dondero, F., Lenzi, A., 'Immunobiology of male infertility' *Hum Reprod* 1988; 3: 75–7

10 Flickinger, C. J., Herr, J. C., Howards, S. S., *et al.*, 'Early testicular changes after vasectomy and vasovasostomy in Lewis rats' *Anat Rec* 1990; 227: 37–46

11 Flickinger, C. J., Howards, S. S., Carey, P. O., *et al.*, 'Testicular alterations are linked to the presence of elevated antisperm antibodies in Sprague–Dawley rats after vasectomy and vasovasostomy' *J Urol* 1988; 140: 627–31

12 Rommerts, F. F. G., 'Testosterone: An overview of biosynthesis, transport, metabolism and action' in Nieschlag, E., Behre, H. M., eds, *Testosterone: Action, deficiency, substitution*. Heidelberg: Springer Verlag, 1990; 1–22

13 Petty, R., 'Serum testosterone, vasectomy and erectile dysfunction: A study' *RCGP Members Reference Handbook*, 1995; 281–3

14 Fawcett, D. W., Howards, S. S., Kisker, T., Alexander, N., Clarksen, T. B., *Vasectomy: Immunologic and pathophysiologic effects in animals*

and man. New York: Academic Press, 1979

15 Glavind, K., Lauritsen, N. R., Klove-Mogensen, M., Carl, J., 'The effect of vasectomy on the production of plasma luteinizing hormone and follicle stimulating hormone in man' *Int Urol Nephrol* 1990; 22: 553–9

16 Peng, X. S., Li, F. D., Miao, Z. R., *et al.*, 'Plasma reproductive hormones in normal and vasectomized Chinese males' *Int J Androl* 1987; 10: 471–9

17 John, E., *et al.*, 'Vasectomy and prostate cancer: Results from a multiethnic case-control study' *Journal of the National Cancer Institute* 1995; 87 – N 9: 662–9

18 Strader, C. H., Weiss, N. S., Daling, J. R., 'Vasectomy and the incidence of testicular cancer' *Am J Epidemiol* 1988; 128: 56–63

19 Cale, A. R., Farouk, M., Prescott, R. J., Wallace, I. W., 'Does vasectomy accelerate testicular tumour? Importance of testicular examinations before and after vasectomy' *BMJ* 1990; 300: 370

20 Thornhill, J. A., Conroy, R. M., Kelly, D. G., Walsh, A., Fennelly, J. J., Fitzpatrick, J. M., 'An evaluation of predisposing factors for testis cancer in Ireland' *Eur Urol* 1988; 14: 429–33

21 Nienhuis, H., Goldacre, M., Seagroatt, V., Gill, L., Vessey, M., 'Incidence of disease after vasectomy: A record linkage retrospective cohort study' *BMJ* 1992; 304: 743–6

22 Brown, L. M., Pottern, L. M., Hoover, R. N., 'Testicular cancer in young men: The search for causes of the epidemic increase in the United States' *J Epidemiol Community Health* 1987; 41: 349–54

23 Toppari, J., *et al.*, 'Male reproductive health and environmental chemicals with estrogenic effects' Miljoprojekt 1995; 290: 1–166

24 Rosenberg, L., Palmer, J. R., Zauber, A. G., Warshauer, M. E., Stolley, P. D., Shapiro, S., 'Vasectomy and the risk of prostate cancer' *American Journal of Epidemiology* 1990; 132: 1051–5

25 Peng, *et al.*, op. cit.

26 Møller, J., Einfeldt, H., *Testosterone Treatment of Cardiovascular Diseases*. Berlin: Springer Verlag, 1984

27 Howard, A. N., Patelski, J., Bowyer, D. E., Gresham, G. A., 'Atherosclerosis induced in hypercholesterolaemic by immunological injury; and the effects of intravenous polyunsaturated phosphatidyl choline' *Atherosclerosis* 1971; 14: 17–29

28 Alexander, N. J., Clarkson, T. B., 'Vasectomy increases the severity of diet-induced atherosclerosis in *Macaca fascicularis*' *Science* 1978; 201: 538–41

29 Anderson, K. M., Wilson, P. W., Garrison, R. J., Castelli, W. P., 'Longitudinal and secular trends in lipoprotein cholesterol measurements in a general population sample' The Framingham Offspring Study. *Atherosclerosis* 1987; 68: 59–66

30 Chi, I. C., Kong, S. K., Wilkens, L. R., *et al.*, 'Vasectomy and cardiovascular deaths in Korean men: A community-based case-control study' *Int J Epidemiol* 1990; 19: 1113–15

31 Petitti, D. B., Klein, R., Kipp, H., Friedman, G. D., 'Vasectomy and the incidence of hospitalized illness' *J Urol* 1983; 129: 760–2

32 Forti, G., Selli, C., 'Prospects for prostatic cancer incidence and treatment by the year 2000' *Int J Androl* 1996; 19: 1–10

33 Møller, op. cit.

34 Nienhuis, *et al.*, op. cit.

35 Forti, op. cit.

36 McDonald, S. W., 'Vasectomy and the human testis: We still know too little about the effects of

vasectomy' Editorial, *BMJ* 1990; 301: 618–19

37 Cooper, A. P., *Observations on the Structure and Diseases of the Testis*. London: Longman, 1831; 51

Chapter Six:
Testosterone Replacement Therapy (TRT)

1 Forti, G., Selli, C., 'Prospects for prostatic cancer incidence and treatment by the year 2000' *Int J Androl* 1996; 19: 1–10

2 Rommerts, F. F. G., 'Testosterone: An overview of biosynthesis, transport, metabolism and action' in Nieschlag, E., Behre, H. M., eds, *Testosterone: Action, deficiency, substitution*. Heidelberg: Springer Verlag, 1990; 1–22

3 Joran, V. C., Murphy, C. S., 'Endocrine pharmacology of antiestrogens as antitumor agents' *Endocr Rev* 1990; 11: 578–610

4 Howell, A., DeFriend, D., Robertson, J., Blamey, R., Walton, P., 'Response to a specific antioestrogen (ICI 182780) in tamoxifen resistant breast cancer' *Lancet* 1995; 345: 29–30

5 Toppari, J., *et al.*, 'Male reproductive health and environmental chemicals with estrogenic effects' 1995; Miljoprojekt 290: 1–166

6 Nieschlag, E., Behre, H. M., 'Pharmacology and clinical uses of testosterone' in Nieschlag, E., Behre, H. M., eds, *Testosterone: Action, deficiency, substitution*. Heidelberg: Springer Verlag, 1990; 92–114

7 Heller, C. G., Myers, G. B., 'The male climacteric: Its symptomatology, diagnosis and treatment' *JAMA* 1944; 126: 472–77

8 Møller, J., Einfeldt, H., *Testosterone Treatment of Cardiovascular Diseases*. Berlin: Springer Verlag, 1984

9 Nieschlag, op. cit.

10 Handelsman, D. J., 'Pharmacology of testosterone pellet implants' in Nieschlag, E., Behre, H. M., eds, *Testosterone: Action, deficiency, substitution*. Heidelberg: Springer Verlag, 1990; 136–54

11 Jayle, M. F., 'In memoriam. Percutaneous absorption of steroids' in Mauvais-Jarvis, P., Vickers, C. F., Wepierre, J., eds, London: Academic Press, 1980; 273–83

12 Delanoe, D., Fougeyrollas, B., Meyer, L., Thonneau, P., 'Androgenisation of female partners of men on medroxyprogesterone acetate/percutaneous testosterone contraception' *Lancet* 1984; 4: 276–7

13 Place, V. A., Atkinson, L., Prather, D. A., Trunnell, N., Yates, F. E., 'Transdermal testosterone replacement through genital skin' in Nieschlag, E., Behre, H. M., eds, *Testosterone: Action, deficiency, substitution*. Heidelberg: Springer Verlag, 1990; 165–81

14 Bals-Pratsch, M., Knuth, U. A., Yoon, Y., Nieschlag, E., 'Transdermal testosterone substitution therapy for male hypogonadism' *Lancet* 1986; 2: 943–6

15 Mazer, N. S., *et al.*, 'Mimicking the circadian pattern of testosterone and metabolite levels with an enhanced transdermal delivery system' in Gurney, Junjinges, Peppas, eds, *Pulsatile Drug Delivery: Current applications and future trends*. Stuttgart: Niss. Verl. Ges. 1993; 73–97

16 Vermeulen, A., 'Androgens and male senescence' in Nieschlag, E., Behre, H. M., eds, *Testosterone: Action, deficiency, substitution*. Heidelberg: Springer Verlag, 1990; 261–76

17 Korkia, P., Stimson, G. V., *Anabolic Steroid Use in Great Britain: An exploratory investigation*. London: HMSO, 1993

18 Wu, F. C., 'Suppression of sperm function by depot

medroxyprogesterone acetate and testosterone enanthate in steroid male contraception' *Fertil Steril* 1989; 51: 691–8

19 Brendler, H., 'Endocrine regulation of prostatic growth' in Engle, E. T., Pincus, G., eds, *Hormones and the Aging Process*. New York: Academic Press Inc., 1956; 273

20 Schroder, F. H., 'Androgens and carcinoma of the prostate' in Nieschlag, E., Behre, H. M., eds, *Testosterone: Action, deficiency, substitution*. Heidelberg: Springer Verlag, 1990; 245–60

21 Sheehy, G., *The Silent Passage*. New York: Random House, 1993

Chapter Seven: Sexual Satisfaction

1 Bancroft, J., *Human Sexuality and its Problems*. Edinburgh: Churchill Livingstone, 1989

2 Ibid.

3 Toone, B. K., Wheeler, M., Nanjee, N., Fenwick, P., Grant, R., 'Sex hormones, sexual activity and plasma anticonvulsant levels in male epileptics' *Journal of Neurology, Neurosurgery and Psychiatry* 1983; 46: 824–6

4 Fenwick, P. B., Mercer, S., Grant, R., *et al.*, 'Nocturnal penile tumescence and serum testosterone levels' *Archives of Sexual Behaviour* 1986; 15: 13–22

5 Martin, L. M., 'Treatment of male sexual dysfunction with sex therapy' in Montague, D. K., ed., *Year Book 1988*. Chicago: Year Book Medical Publishers, 1988; 142–53

6 Masters, W. H., Johnson, V. E., *Human Sexual Inadequacy*. London: Churchill, 1970

7 Bancroft, op. cit.

8 Heller, C. G., Myers, G. B., 'The male climacteric:
   Its symptomatology, diagnosis and treatment'
   JAMA 1944; 126: 472-77

9 Huws, R., 'Antihypertensive medication and sexual
   problems' in Riley, A. J., Peet, M., Wilson, C., eds,
   Sexual Pharmacology. Oxford: Oxford University
   Press, 1993; 146–58

10 Barnes, T. R. E., Harvey. C. A., 'Psychiatric drugs
    and sexuality' in Riley, A. J., Peet, M., Wilson, C.,
    eds, *Sexual Pharmacology*. Oxford: Oxford University
    Press, 1993; 176–96

11 Kaplan, H. S,. *Disorders of Sexual Desire*. New York:
    Brunner Mazel Inc., 1979

12. Gomaa A., *et al.*, Topical cream for erectile
     dysfunction: Randomised, double–blind placebo
     controlled trial of cream containing ammophylline,
     isosorbide dinitrate and co-dergocrine mesylate.
     BMJ 1996; 312: 1512–15

Chapter Eight: Secrets of Vitality and Virility

1 Carruthers, M., 'Hormone replacement therapy for
   men' *RCGP Members Reference Book* 1993; 283–5

2 Carruthers, M., *The Western Way of Death: Stress,
   tension and heart disease*. London and New York:
   Davis-Poynter and Pantheon Books, 1974

3 Carruthers, M., 'Hypothesis: Aggression and
   atheroma' *Lancet* 1969; 2: 1170–1

4 Taggart, P., Parkinson, P., Carruthers, M. E., 'Cardiac
   responses to thermal, physical and emotional stress'
   British Medical Journal 1972; 3: 71–6

5 Carruthers, M. E., Taggart, P., 'Endogenous
   hyperlipidaemia induced by stress of racing driving'
   Lancet 1971; 1: 363–6

6 Friedman, M., Rosenman, R. H. *Type-A Behaviour*

and your Heart. New York, Alfred A. Knopf, 1972

7 Carter, J., *Nasty People: How to stop being hurt by them without becoming one of them*. Chicago: Contemporary Books, 1989

8 Byrne, E., *The Games People Play*. New York: Pantheon, 1974

9 Carruthers and Taggart, op. cit.

10 Ibid.

11 Poteliakhoff, A., Carruthers, M., *Real Health: The ill effects of stress and their prevention*. London: Davis-Poynter, 1981

12 Carruthers, M., Murray, A., *F/40: Fitness on Forty Minutes a Week*. London: Futura, 1976

13 Carruthers, M. E., 'Exercise programmes: The European experience' *British Journal of Sport and Medicine* 1979; 12: 235–40

14 Taggart, Parkinson and Carruthers, op. cit.

15 Carruthers, M., 'Voluntary control of the involuntary nervous system: Comparison of Autogenic Training and siddha meditation' in McGuigan, M. J., Sime, W. E., and Macdonald Wallace, J., eds, *Stress and Tension Control*. New York and London: Plenum Press, 1979; 267–75

16 Luthe, W., *Autogenic Therapy: Research and theory*. New York and London: Grune and Stratton, 1970

17 Carruthers, M. E., 'Autogenic Training' *J Psychosom Res* 1979; 23: 437–40

18 Hayes, P., *The Supreme Adventure*. London: Thorsons, 1995

19 Muktananda, S., *Meditate*. Albany: State University of New York Press, 1980

Index